Roz Shafran is Professor of Translational Psychology at UCL Great Ormond Street Institute of Child Health. She is a clinical psychologist and has extensive clinical and research expertise in cognitive behavioural theory and treatment of psychological disorders across the age range. She has co-authored three self-help books and one edited book including *Overcoming Perfectionism*, *The CBT Handbook* and *The Complete CBT Guide for Anxiety*; she has written over 250 peer-reviewed publications. She has three children.

Ursula Saunders is a fundraiser in the charity sector. Previously she worked for Radio 4 as a researcher and producer. She has two children.

Alice Welham is a clinical psychologist and a lecturer at the University of Leicester. She has a broad range of interests in psychology and its clinical applications and has published research in a number of areas. She has two children.

T0003631

Roz Shafran, Ursula Saunders
and Alice Welham

How
to
Cope

WHEN YOUR CHILD CAN'T

Comfort, Help &
Hope for Parents

ROBINSON

ROBINSON

First published in Great Britain in 2022 by Robinson

3 5 7 9 10 8 6 4

Important Note

This book is not intended as a substitute for medical advice or treatment.
Any person with a condition requiring medical attention should consult
a qualified medical practitioner or suitable therapist.

A CIP catalogue record for this book
is available from the British Library.

ISBN: 978-1-47213-901-6

Typeset in Times by Initial Typesetting Services, Edinburgh
Printed and bound in Great Britain by Clays Ltd, Elcograf S.p.A.

Papers used by Robinson are from well-managed forests and
other responsible sources.

Robinson
An imprint of
Little, Brown Book Group
Carmelite House
50 Victoria Embankment
London EC4Y 0DZ

An Hachette UK Company
www.hachette.co.uk

www.littlebrown.co.uk

To our parents and children

Contents

SECTION 4: IT WORKED FOR ME – TOP TIPS FROM PEOPLE WHO HAVE BEEN THROUGH IT

SECTION 5: ACCEPTANCE

Preface

It is often said that 'You are only as happy as your unhappiest child'. But what happens when that's not very happy at all? Many children experience significant periods of distress, including anxiety, sadness, anger and more. Some children have serious mental health challenges, others have social challenges like being left out or being bullied. For some, periods of unhappiness might relate to physical disabilities, learning challenges or having to manage visible differences. For many, parenting is a lifelong challenge.

It can be heart-breaking to watch your child suffering and struggling to cope with the demands of life. We suffer alongside them. We might try to 'be strong' for them, and to hide our despair in front of them, and then cry, rage and worry in private. Parenting a child who isn't managing well can be extremely challenging, both physically and mentally. And it may not be the only thing going on at home. Life can be extremely messy. Illness, divorce, financial worries, professional woes, bereavements – the list goes on. Major life events generally do not come at easy or appropriate times. So how can we get by? How do we cope when our child can't? This book tries to answer that question.

We know from our combined professional and personal experiences just how hard it can be to function when your child is unhappy. Between us we have seven children. Two of us are clinical psychologists and one of us is a fundraiser. We have pooled our knowledge and experiences, together with those of many other parents, to work out what has helped us all, across a variety of situations. We spoke with parents who, despite many other challenges, slept in their children's rooms for months, to try to protect them from self-harming. We spoke with parents whose child never had a friend to play with at break-time, parents whose child was struggling with the effects of a genetic condition, and parents whose child was just 'different'. We have spoken with parents whose child took their own life. Parenting children when they're struggling can be an incredibly difficult, frightening, exhausting and sometimes thankless task. Often all the energy in the household becomes focused on the child that is struggling. It becomes very easy to neglect ourselves at every level.

We've also spoken with parents – the same parents – who have found or are finding a way through. Parents who have experienced the depths of despair and discovered that they are still themselves; still able to find meaning and pleasure in life, when at one stage that had seemed impossible. For the purposes of the book, we have changed the names and details of everyone who has been brave enough to share their story. We have sometimes created illustrations based on our collective personal and professional experiences.

The goal of the book is to combine people's experiences with psychological research and clinical experience to bring comfort, help and hope.

- **Comfort –** You are not alone. Unfortunately, pressures on children have increased for many reasons, including social media and academic pressures. According to UNICEF, in 2019, it was estimated that one in seven adolescents experience mental health conditions. This amounts to an estimated 175 million adolescent boys and girls globally, an increase of about 4 million since 2000. And that's before counting all the children whose difficulties don't fit into the category of specific mental health difficulties. In any case, the statistics are one thing. Living with a child who is sad, worried, anxious, angry or has any other type of emotional or behavioural problem is another. It can lead to feelings of despair, loneliness, grief and shame and sometimes a strong sense that you have failed as a parent, that nobody understands what it is like to be you. We hope knowing you are not alone will bring comfort.

- **Help** – The exercises, suggestions and strategies in the book have been chosen from research and experience. This is not intended to be a book mainly about self-care, or managing your own mental health problems, or improving your child's well-being or behaviour directly through parenting programmes. There are lots of other books out there and we have a Further resources section on problems such as depression or anxiety, which includes some information about parenting books. We know that what can be really useful is hearing from others who have been in the same situation and come out the other side. For that reason, the book has plenty of case illustrations. We also include a chapter on 'top tips' based on those provided by the real experts – parents who have lived through what you are going through and wanted to share their experiences.

- **Hope** – The people for whom things have got better, whose lives have been improved with the help of these strategies, have shared their experiences. 'Hope is Strong' is one of the mantras referred to in one of our case studies. People have generously shared their stories to give hope to those of us who are going through those dark times right now.

Introduction

The problem

Internet searches for how to survive, cope and – dare we say it – even feel some happiness despite your child being sad reveal very little. It is a taboo subject. There is plenty online about how to help your 'unhappy' child but helping parents through the misery of these situations is an oddly neglected area. That is the gap we hope to fill with this book.

In writing this, it has often been difficult to untangle the 'what helps you' information from 'what helps your child', and there are obvious overlaps.

Many of the parents we spoke to, when asked what helped them cope, initially answered with a raft of suggestions and creative ideas all focused on what best helped their child. It often took a second or third attempt to get them to focus on *their* potential happiness and coping strategies, involving experiences and outlets that usually did not involve their child. It was as if permission to focus on ourselves was both impossible and forbidden.

Of course, one of the lines that runs through our research and this book, is that if we can manage to help ourselves a little, the improvement in our mental health may impact positively on our ability to help our children. Taking care of yourself is what we're constantly told we should do: we know all about 'not pouring from an empty cup', and 'putting on your own lifejacket and oxygen mask before attempting to help anyone else'.

But how? How do we find a moment to even find the lifejacket amidst the overwhelming demands of caring and safeguarding and comforting? There is also potential interplay between the mood and behaviour of a parent and that of their child. We can become impatient, frustrated and angry, which often makes a bad situation worse. So, it is in everyone's best interests to try and find the best ways to cope ourselves.

Another phrase we hear often is: '*All I want is for them to be happy.*' The more we are exposed to the complications of our children's lives, the more we realise, as parents, that this is indeed a worthy goal, but by no means an easy one. There's no '*all*' about it.

So, we need to find ways of coping and feeling resilient, even when our children are not happy.

Coping will of course mean different things to different people at different times. For some, coping could be simply getting up in the morning, getting washed, dressed, eating. It may simply be that if you are breathing, then you are coping. There may be more lightness on other days: the pleasure of finishing a small task, or a flash of humour or joy. And on some days, none of the above will even register. Often coping may be facing – literally, looking in the face – your distress, worry, anxiety, sadness or your own loss of control, and seeing that you can tolerate these things, pick yourself up and carry on.

We hope this book can help you, no matter the *reasons* your child isn't coping and no matter the precise nature or source of their unhappiness. It might be fear, anger, sadness, eating disorders, self-harm, obsessions, physical illness or disability, problems with physical appearance, bullying, lack of friends, gender identity, sexuality, social media scrutiny, problems with friends, addictions . . . or simply the pressure of life. Perhaps they have a specific diagnosis, many diagnoses or maybe it's been difficult or unhelpful to categorise exactly what's 'wrong'. It could be that this is a new thing for your child, or perhaps it's been going on for as long as you can remember. Perhaps something definite happened, or maybe you can't identify when or how the problem started.

Having a child who is struggling impacts on every area of life. If they are not in school, then that can become extra challenging. If your child is not coping in school, it becomes difficult to work productively and many of the parents we spoke to ended up altering their working lives and sometimes giving up work entirely. This impacts all aspects of family life, including finances, and may dramatically change lives. Social circles can change quickly, with established networks falling away for a variety of reasons.

Our relationships with other members in our family can become strained too. Siblings who witness great unhappiness in their brothers and sisters, and the impact on parents, might be affected in complex ways. They may feel sidelined by mothers and fathers who do not have the capacity to give them the attention they also need. Many parents spoke of their guilt and regrets around parenting their other children who ended up taking second place at times, while the unhappy child took up all the attention. Of course, experiencing other people's struggles is also an inevitable part of life, and can build empathy and resilience, and the effects on siblings may also include these positive aspects.

We have spoken to parents who can look back at periods of great unhappiness (theirs and their children's) and see it in the past. Family dynamics change, children grow up and problems that loomed large at one stage can resolve and settle down over time. Scientists now believe that the adolescent brain continues to mature past the age of eighteen until about twenty-four years old, so 'teenage' years last a lot longer than was previously thought. We heard from parents that they have learned valuable lessons through very difficult years, making them less judgemental as people, better friends and more compassionate members of society. Importantly, there are of course circumstances and situations that cannot be changed in themselves. What can be changed is your reaction to your child, and how you manage and accept the various challenges that will be presented.

What the book covers

The book is divided into five sections. The first shares personal stories from a range of parents who have managed to survive their child's distress and even their child's suicide. The second focuses on untangling yourself from your child. The third describes strategies from psychological research that have been shown to be useful in managing mood, situations and behaviour. The fourth provides additional strategies that parents have used and their 'top tips'. The final section addresses the difficult idea of acceptance.

What the book doesn't cover

We want to be clear that this is not a book on managing mental health problems that you may have, such as depression or anxiety (although it might help with these things too). There are many other great books available for that. Nor is it a book on 'well-being' – a simple internet search of 'five ways to well-being' will give a wealth of helpful ideas. But making sure you get enough sleep, food, exercise – the basics – is fundamental and their importance shouldn't be forgotten.

How to make best use of the book

We have all bought books that promise a lot in the title, and then remain unread and daunting on our bookshelves – as if the action of buying the book is enough. Diet books are a classic case in point. But we want this book to be the opposite of daunting – a compassionate, non-judgemental friend of a book.

Some may wish to go through the book chapter by chapter, doing the exercises diligently and over a concentrated period of time. For others, a quote or phrase from another parent who has experienced something similar will provide a glimmer of comfort or hope, and help just a little in a very dark moment.

It may be that you prefer to dip in and out, or pick and choose the chapters that mean most to you. You may know a lot about some areas – and wish to skim those chapters – but less about others. Some of the chapters may annoy you. For example, we have a chapter on setting boundaries. For those who have tried and found it hasn't worked, please just skip over that chapter. But it may be useful for others and give some practical ways to untangle yourself from your child. We know that no two people, families or situations are the same and we want you to personalise how you use the book so it fits best with your own situation.

We do not believe that this book is some kind of magic happiness pill, or that after reading it you will suddenly be able to cope brilliantly all the time with the challenges of life and your child. But however you use it, we hope that you find something that brings comfort, help and hope.

SECTION 1:
TRUE STORIES TO GIVE
COMFORT, HELP AND HOPE

1: True stories

When we set out to write this book, the first thing we did was speak with others who had experienced some of the many challenges of parenting children when they were unhappy, who had struggled to cope.

We spoke with a range of parents about what situations they had found themselves in and how they had managed themselves and their families through the hardest of times. As mentioned earlier, it was sometimes hard to untangle what helped them from what helped their child, but common themes did begin to emerge. They all felt that taking time to think about their own well-being and what had helped them was worthwhile and important to share.

Christina

Christina is the mother in a family unit of four which includes her husband and a fifteen-year-old son. Her now eighteen-year-old daughter, Evie, had originally been placed on the autism spectrum but also had severe anorexia. As her mental health deteriorated during her teenage years, Evie self-harmed and made suicide attempts. At one stage she was sectioned, ending up in a secure unit several hours away from home.

As a child, Evie was bright, unusual and very active. Christina looks back with incredulity at the schedule of activities that they kept up. But these were a distraction for Evie – a way of managing her energy. Evie, who 'never fitted the mould' was bullied throughout her early school years and the attempt to solve this through moving schools only worked for a while.

When Evie developed anorexia, it was a highly visible condition. Christina realised that the 'external front' which they had previously kept up was just that: it could not be hidden behind closed doors. 'We were failing, publicly, as parents.' So began an insight into a world that was incredibly lonely and extreme. 'There is a whole world out there that you have no idea exists until you become part of it. We watched our daughter held down in a room where there was nothing but a mattress. She was unsafe in any other setting.' During another period, Christina stayed with her daughter night and day for three months in an attempt to stop her coming to harm.

The whole family suffered. 'The isolation was overwhelming.' Christina's son witnessed his parents and sister going through periods of real desperation. 'He saw things no child should have seen at his age.' Her husband, the main breadwinner, was working in a very stressful job and, as a couple, they had 'some really dreadful periods' – it was difficult to keep their relationship on track. Christina felt that her own mental health was slipping.

Despite her education being sporadic, Evie has been able to build on her talents and has kept a pulse on getting formal qualifications. When her daughter has been away – in hospital, for instance – Christina has taken the opportunity to focus on her son, giving him maximum time and attention, and this has been a very positive experience. She and her husband, even at their lowest, have remembered that they do love each other, and they always come back to this. Over time, Christina has found value in not being on 'the treadmill' of a more normal family life. Spontaneity began to feature more in their lives – for instance if they felt like going to the beach, they would. Making quick decisions on the spur of the moment took them away from the world of planning and gave them energy (even when they couldn't follow through with the idea).

Christina has been able to keep working at her job (gardening), even though there have been times when it has slipped to just a day a week. It has given her some life outside and a chance to keep up something she is good at. Her employer has been incredibly supportive, allowing her to change her hours according to family circumstances. There has also been happiness and peace in walking the dog: Christina joined a group and found people who were non-judgemental and rarely talked about families at all. At one point, she became a dog-walker.

Christina never found online support helpful and has not sought it out. On the other hand, because of her daughter's struggles, Christina has discovered some deep and honest friendships, relationships that perhaps would never have happened if life had been more mainstream. Her world view has broadened and she now 'sees life through a different lens', having a different set of values and expectations. Some mantras have been empowering: 'Hope is strong', 'Find good in each day' and (a bit tougher!) 'If you lie on a rock for ten years, you get used to it'.

Strategies for coping with Evie have developed. Christina has become good at pausing, realising that there are times when it is better to let Evie 'sit with her sadness' rather than trying to drag her out of it. This was part of letting go of control, to some extent, accepting that she couldn't manage every detail of her daughter's mental health. Conversely some simple interventions have been very satisfying, like cultivating playfulness. 'When my daughter was at her lowest, she would respond to very silly, cute things, so

I would text her pictures of ducklings or piglets – the cuter the better. Sometimes I would dress up to amuse her – tiny injections of humour into her very bleak world.' They also went back to reading children's books and watching movies they had watched when Evie was much smaller. Christina found an emotional simplicity and nurture in these things.

What helped

- Sitting with sadness
- Injections of humour and silliness
- Friends and work outside
- Trying to think differently and see life through a different lens

Ife

Ife has three children: one with a diagnosis of borderline personality disorder, one with autism and the third struggling at having to take on a 'caring' role. With hindsight, she now believes that her former husband (they separated ten years ago) is also on the spectrum – but 'it would have been culturally taboo to consider an ASD diagnosis for him'.

Although the father remains partially in their lives, the children are not helped by 'a lot of erratic and unreasonable behaviour' that he shows, mainly exhibiting as impatience. Ife herself is part of a strong family group, with a particularly supportive and helpful mother, but the family has suffered recently from the death of Ife's younger sister. The children have had to have numerous hospital interventions. She remembers a consultant, who was looking after the daughter in hospital, saying to her, we are the doctors, but you are the expert on your child. Ife felt that this was an endorsement of something she knew deep down, something she had to hang on to.

Ife's response to the problems she faces has hinged on a determination to confront them. In order to get a better understanding of the situation in which she finds herself, she has successfully taken a Master's degree in Mental Health.

Although she is 'not a fan of organised religion', spiritual health has always been very important. Her own deep faith and the idea that 'everything happens for a reason' have also strengthened her belief in herself. Since her sister's death, she has changed her idea of happiness as a sort of euphoria to seeing it as more bound up with an idea of peace. She seeks out 'peaceful moments', which she manages to notice and enjoy. She also consciously credits her family and friends as an important blessing in her life.

Empowering herself with knowledge of mental health issues has really helped. Ife has fought for her own children's rights, through tribunals and the court system. She has worked in a school, helping traumatised children, and feels that improving the lives of her own children and of other parents who do not have her own confidence and voice has, in a way, been part of a coping mechanism for herself.

What helped

- Studying to gain knowledge and insight into the situation
- Building on a spiritual strength
- Gratitude for friends and family and taking them as a blessing
- Taking advantage of whatever help is on offer

Lola

Lola is the mother of two boys. The younger one, Daniel, has always struggled out of the home. He has suffered from loneliness and bullying at school. Her husband is a generally supportive but rather distant and 'hands off' father. She also feels that her husband's family do little to help.

The COVID-19 pandemic brought Lola's problems to the fore. She had to spend time 'shielding', thanks to an underlying health condition. Although 'lockdown' suited Daniel quite well, that was temporary, and his older brother found the restrictions placed on him extremely difficult.

Recently, Lola remembered something from several years ago. She had, in a very honest way, confronted her mother-in-law over a period of prolonged bullying, spanning many years. What she remembered was that the next day, after the conversation, she had slept right through the school run, such was her sense of exhaustion and release. She resolved to nurture a positive outlook in herself and her children and to build on her own strengths.

During the first coronavirus lockdown, Lola joined an online choir and felt that it was a great outlet. She also used the extra time to tidy up the garden – and found herself really appreciating the benefits of having a garden. In addition, there was time to pursue her love of practical arts and crafts; things which keep her culturally grounded.

Most importantly, Lola has rethought her whole attitude to her family:

> 'It is similar to having children with additional needs and when these needs were not expected we, as parents, have to rethink our imagined futures for them. Yes, they will hopefully all go and have a great future in whatever field makes them happy, but it will be different to our unspoken parental expectations when they first burst into the world.'

Focusing on her younger son, in particular, Lola is determined to reduce his sense of isolation and loneliness and help him to build up his social skills – in particular by nurturing his primary school friendships.

What helped

- Clearing the air with an honest conversation
- Singing in a choir
- Using skills to make things
- Nurturing friendships

Amanda

Amanda is the mother of two girls – Dora (sixteen) and Jenna (fourteen). She is married and the relationship is strong. Before having children, Amanda worked in group management and describes herself as 'relatively thick-skinned and confident'. Jenna, who has a diagnosis of epilepsy as well as autism and ADHD, does not go to school.

Jenna has been out of school for the past three years. From when she was seven or eight years old, her parents tried to get her into various schools and educational settings, which left Jenna 'traumatised'. Amanda says that it has sometimes been a struggle for both parents to stay aligned in their responses. 'I think of it like this: Jenna is like a pack of huskies and I am attached by a very short rope whereas my husband is on a long elastic. So, he gets further and further behind and then suddenly slams into the back of us and gets himself back up to speed.'

Amanda is aware that she has some personal attributes which help her to cope: 'I can manage other people's scathing and judgemental attitudes'. She reckons that, as an eldest child, she was the one with the most self-confidence and now she doesn't really mind what other people think of her.

Online support has been a lifeline for the family as a whole. Amanda has delved into Jenna's diagnoses and has found supportive communities. '"Not Fine In School" has been a particularly valuable website.' The research means that Amanda now has a network of autistic adults that she can consult from time to time. This way she can frame Jenna's situation through different – often more relevant – eyes and can get help and an alternative way of interpreting things. She describes this as 'new ways of making it through the mazes'.

Amanda is a convert to mindfulness. Spending time outside and within the natural world allows 'an essential slowing-down' to take place. This can be combined with Jenna's love of animals – as a result they have lots of family pets.

Every year, Amanda insists on having a few days away from the family, with a group of friends. She admits that this must be 'hellish' for her husband but identifies it as a survival strategy and has safeguarded this week over the years.

What helped

- Doing online research and advice
- A network of 'experts' to consult
- Pets
- Mindfulness within nature
- An occasional break, away from the family

Ali

Ali is a single parent to Josh, now aged eighteen. She had never really wanted children and Josh was 'unplanned'. He started school refusing when he was about thirteen. At first this problem seemed to come 'out of the blue' but Ali remembers that she had been a very difficult teenager herself.

1: True stories

When Josh started to refuse to go to school, Ali felt that she could not possibly leave an unhappy thirteen-year-old alone at home. This meant that she had to make a radical change in how she worked. She became freelance and gave up the security and sociability of an office. This was also a move with financial implications.

Ali also had to rethink her whole attitude to life. She felt 'a huge sense of bereavement and loss' and there were layers of guilt to pick through. She did not want advice and help from others – 'in fact, it made me mad'. She tends to reject concepts of 'sad' versus 'happy', reckoning that 'mostly life is lived in the middle lane'.

Ali chose not to seek out online support or external help. She real-ised that she had the ability to 'sit with it', take a longer view and rely on hope. She was comfortable giving Josh 'time to go through whatever he was going through. I could allow it to run its course, not rushing it.' Ali says: 'I saw in the complexity of his difficulties a lot of goodness and at times thought maybe it's OK to have this struggle. Josh is becoming a more complex and wise person and will definitely have more compassion.'

Ali realised early on that she had to 'pick her battles' with Josh. For example, she allowed him to sleep in in the mornings so that she could give herself time for a daily swim. This meant that he got up later than she would have wanted but the swim made her feel better and gave her physical interaction with others, out in the world.

Getting outside, into nature, was also important. Ali persisted with Josh, starting with small steps – one or two minutes, a couple of times a week at first has built up to daily walks for them both over the years. Ali found a great release in gardening – 'the feeling that I could make things grow and thrive was a profound one.'

'Not being the mother' has led to another path for Ali. She has been able to connect with the daughter of a friend in a different way from the mother and offer non-judgemental support, which has helped both of them. In fact, 'valuing the strength and currency of relationships, of other people who can listen, again without judgement, has been one of the great positives.'

What helped

- Taking a long view and relying on hope
- Picking battles
- Gardening and walking
- Connecting with someone else's child

Brigid

Brigid is the mother of three children, Hannah being the youngest. Hannah now lives, with a young son, a few miles away from her parents and both parents help her out daily. All three children have had had their difficulties, but Hannah's have been the most difficult to handle.

In her early teens, Hannah suffered badly with acne. She was always particularly sensitive, worrying about the planet 'long before anyone else did'. She was academically strong and seemed set on a successful career in work connected with the natural world. Hannah moved abroad to pursue her career, but her life was cyclical, with successes followed by periods when she came crashing down. At one point she had a car crash, which led to several operations and a lot of pain. In her late twenties, Hannah was diagnosed with bipolar II disorder. Brigid and her husband found it very difficult to care for their daughter, living in a different country. Eventually Hannah returned, pregnant, and settled back in the UK, as a single mum.

1: True stories

Brigid worries about how things might have been different. The early problem with acne coincided with a period of ill-health for Brigid – did this impact particularly badly on Hannah at this time? And there were times when both parents wished they had changed schools for their daughter – perhaps that would have made a profound difference to Hannah's happiness in those years?

Brigid also wonders about her own decision to keep working throughout Hannah's difficulties. She realised that it was an escape and outlet for her, describing her work as 'safeguarding her life'. It came with stresses of its own but gave her respite at times, and other people to think about. However, when dealing with other people's difficulties as part of her job and then going home to her own difficult family life, 'it could all become very toxic'.

Gradually, Brigid is starting to find solutions and positives in her life. Importantly, she has a strategy of trying to consciously recognise what is going well, which often involves looking at the broader picture. 'It is very easy to get caught up in the minutiae of dreadful periods, but the broader picture is often less grim.' For instance, Brigid can see the value that her family as a whole bring to the world. The two older children now both have jobs in caring professions. They have not followed the 'successful' routes of many of their contemporaries, but she is very proud of the value that they bring to the world as it is.

Brigid has tackled recurring regrets by taking on the mantra of 'You are doing the best that you can'. It has helped because it tackles guilt and expectations of what family life could or should be. She also looks at this mantra from her children's perspective, understanding that they are not being deliberately unhappy and difficult, that they too are doing their best. A cycle of unproductive rumination can be recognised as such and turned into something proactive and problem-solving. Brigid started to outsource. 'I gave myself permission. It wasn't my job to do everything.'

Friendship is important, but it is not always as easy as it sounds. It is often hard to connect with peers whose children are of a similar age, as comparisons and contrasts can bite more keenly. Brigid has recognised that friends need to be non-judgemental and imaginative. She now finds support from colleagues and friends of all ages.

When the children were young, Brigid introduced the concept of 'family meetings', which became quite formalised (with a 'talking stick') and have continued into adulthood. They give everyone a chance to have their say, and a clear 'agenda' helps in broaching difficult topics while making everyone feel safe and contained. With her husband Brigid realised that they needed to focus on shared goals and work together, rather than sniping about what each had done wrong. This has been a conscious strategy in that they can now see what each of them brings to the partnership.

She also notes that doing things together with Hannah helped, whether watching the same TV programme, cooking together or making things (Christmas cards was one shared pleasure each year). A distracting or absorbing focus gave their relationship a nice conduit for positive time together.

What helped

- Recalibrating goals and expectations
- Outsourcing some responsibilities
- Having a variety of friends
- Shared tasks/occupations, e.g., cooking together, crafting together, watching a TV programme together

- Setting up shared goals within the family
- The mantra 'you are doing the best that you can'

Tess

Two of Tess's three children have been diagnosed, relatively late, as being on the autistic spectrum and Tess now thinks she too has aspects of ASD. Looking back, she reckons that she herself was brought up very rigidly and strictly. She has struggled since her children were of secondary school age and started to school refuse.

The children's school refusal has been very difficult for Tess. One of her boys has been mute for periods of time and the frustrations that they all experience can lead to violent outbursts, with family life becoming fraught. School refusal takes a terrible toll on work patterns and Tess has to cut back on her commitments in order to be at home as much as possible.

Tess, generally pragmatic, felt that she had to be quite aggressive in seeking help, which has been difficult to find, and she has not liked having to be aggressive. Some routes offering professional help felt rather judgemental, focused on making her son behave like someone he was not.

Tess persisted with different assessments and diagnostic routes and eventually found one professional who absolutely 'got' her son. This person felt almost magical, 'guru-like', and gave everyone hope. Finding him was initially the most helpful thing for Tess.

Later there was an occupational therapist who was able to explain why certain disruptive behaviours took place and what the roots of that behaviour were. They explained how particular physical activities could help him to regulate his behaviour and why others could result in the hatred he felt for school sports. These insights

21

were crucial. Practical support in the form of occupational therapy showed quick results and changed the energy at home. One particular suggestion, that the boy try climbing, offered particular release and he would come home more 'chilled' than after any other activity.

Tess found some online forums helpful in offering a mix of experiences and suggestions from other parents. She also got herself onto free online conferences whenever possible and learned a lot about autism and the challenges that her children were experiencing. It was at this point that she began to recognise her own autistic traits and so became better able to understand and regulate herself. She found some trauma relief exercises that worked for her mental health but didn't want to follow a full talking therapy; after a couple of sessions with EFT (emotional freedom technique, which can be picked up relatively easily online), she was able to do the exercises herself. Her own self-exploration and reflection on her childhood has enabled her to pull back from that model of parenting which would be disastrous for her children.

Like many parents, Tess succumbed to getting a dog. In fact, it wasn't a great game-changer for her children, but it meant that she got more time outdoors, enjoying nature as well as the exercise. The dog-walking helps her to 'stay in the moment' and avoid, even for a short time, the painful preoccupation of looking ahead for her children.

What helped

- Finding a professional supporter
- Using occupational therapy
- Learning about her specific child's autistic traits
- Walking the dog

Tom

Tom is father to two daughters, Ella and Lily, aged twenty and seventeen. He and his wife separated when the girls were much younger, but they shared the parenting and he played an active role in bringing up Ella in particular. Ella has been given a series of diagnoses, including Asperger's and BPD (borderline personality disorder).

From early secondary school stage, Ella, in particular, struggled with mainstream education and by the age of fourteen, she found it impossible to attend school. She had periods of being mute and being hospitalised and was given the ASD and BPD diagnoses. Tom and his ex-wife found the next four years extremely difficult and painful, especially as they realised that Ella was not suffering from some acute illness that might eventually go away: 'We were in it for the long haul and it was no good looking for quick fixes.'

They decided that their primary job would be to act as essential advocates for Ella. There was a great deal of necessary administration involved in negotiating tribunals and the school and mental health systems. Ella required constant monitoring. They remain her advocates even though Ella is currently living in a shared house and pursuing further education – something neither of them would have dared to hope for even a couple of years ago.

Tom's handling of the difficulties presented by Ella rely on his understanding of himself and his strengths. He is analytical by nature and works with monitoring and evaluating systems and data. 'With his work hat on' he decided to 'project manage' his daughter's situation. 'I fitted it into my day, much as I would an additional work project. This way I could create a bit of fake distance and apply my skills as best as I could.' Tom reckons that taking a

23

dispassionate view helped him to stay in control and, as a result, make better decisions.

With her parents taking control of her mental health, Ella came to trust them and feel that they were clearly on her side. 'We did our best to work with and for her at all times, though it was often difficult.' It was also important to see Ella as 'a daughter, rather than bunch of diagnoses and conditions'. Tom had to learn to listen, to allow Ella to speak, and to really hear her. He found it was much harder than it sounds. At times he was tempted to comment and disagree, which tended to undermine Ella. But as he tried to avoid playing the 'wise adult' role, she started to open up. 'I realised that my tendency to start every sentence with "When I was your age . . ." was actually extremely annoying.'

Ella and Tom bonded over shared interests and attitudes (notably on the Brexit vote and the Trump election!). These interests had been consciously and deliberately fostered at a time when it would have been possible to focus only on Ella's education and mental health. Tom thinks that keeping an external focus on the world helped them both. Humour played a huge role too. They would invent lives for the educators, consultants and therapists they came into contact with. It was a sort of mischief and distraction that helped them to bond at stressful times, giving an emotional, creative release.

Throughout his life, Tom has had periods of keeping a regular journal. By looking back at his own life and the family life, he has been able to reflect carefully, and he credits this self-reflection with enabling him to take a long-term view of Ella's difficulties. 'I have managed my own expectations accordingly. This sounds very simple, but as a strategy it has been incredibly helpful and has kept my own mental health on track through everything.' Tom has tried to keep an adult life, one separate from his parent life (in that respect being separate from the girls' mother has been helpful – they both have valuable times away from the girls). Tom enjoys following his own interests and is not afraid of being alone.

What helped

- Knowing yourself and building on your strengths
- Humour and creative thinking
- Constructive listening
- Keeping up your own interests

Janina

Janina is a mum to two children: her daughter Rasa, eighteen, and her son Elijah, seventeen. Janina used to be a primary school teacher but gave this up when Elijah was a toddler. She started part-time work again last year as an administrator. She is married to the children's father, Ado, who works as a mechanic.

Janina started to notice when Elijah was a baby that he was learning new skills much more slowly than his sister had. He also didn't seem to look much like anyone else in the family. When, at over two years old, he wasn't walking or talking and kept getting ear infections, many medical investigations started. At three Elijah was diagnosed with a rare genetic syndrome which affects his learning and development, his physical health and his appearance. People with this condition often have high rates of anxiety and difficulties with low mood: Elijah suffers from both.

Elijah now goes to a special needs college five days a week, where he has discovered a love of pottery and glass painting. Socialising has often been difficult for him as he gets very anxious about meeting new people (and can sometimes be aggressive when he's anxious). However, he has recently made a friend at college, whom he sometimes rings at weekends. He lives at home with his parents. Rasa has gone to university in another city, to study nursing.

Janina says, 'It was a massive relief' when they finally got Elijah's diagnosis. There was a reason for the problems, so she could stop the tendency to blame herself. And 'there were suddenly people to help us and talk to us'. But they still had to cope with grief and a sense of resentment. Janina quotes a story she's often heard: 'You're expecting a nice warm holiday in Spain. You've packed your sundress and you're looking forward to lying on the beach, swimming and drinking sangria. Then when the plane touches down, you're somewhere you don't recognise – it's cold and there's no beach and the sign says, "Welcome to the Netherlands".' Although this might seem to trivialise the experience of parents in this situation, Janina has come to cherish the story because it rings true to her. After the initial shock you can change your expectations and have a different, but still good, holiday. 'The initial response of "Why us?" can move to "Why not us?" And you can start living again.' Over time both she and Ado have learned to let go of expectations and to accept Elijah for himself. 'There's a joy in small things such as, "He tried a new food!", "He's got a friend!"' Janina reckons that she is a more accepting mother to her daughter as well, no longer feeling that she should be judged by comparisons with others.

Janina and Ado have had to struggle with adjusting to different phases of Elijah's development, but they feel that instead of being overwhelmed by worry about the future they do best with a 'Today Only' mantra. Now, Janina says, 'the hardest thing by far is when Elijah is unhappy, and we can't fix it'. But they have learned that no mood lasts forever and that they can always rely on 'a time when you feel a bit better even if the situation doesn't exactly change'.

Janina reckons that she herself has changed: 'I used to be a very timid person. It turned out that I needed to change that – and it turned out that I could.' She thinks she has grown 'fierce and strong' when having to fight for Elijah – getting him funding, the right college, good medical treatment. Joining support groups and fighting for more funding for children with disabilities has helped Janina connect with other people – all across the world – whose children have a similar genetic condition. She and Ado now get respite care, so they can have a weekend away every few months. ('And you have to learn not to feel guilty about that.') Janina also says to herself 'Life isn't meant to be easy or meant to be any specific way. It just is how it is. Sometimes I can see that now and feel a sense of peace that "whatever happens will happen".'

What helped

- Joining an active support group
- Going away for weekends, using respite care
- Learning to say, 'Why *not* us?'
- Remembering that everything passes, and everything in life is a phase

Mary

Mary is a single parent to Bailey – now an adult. Bailey struggled at school, particularly as he headed into his teenage years, when he self-harmed and, on several occasions, tried to harm both himself and Mary.

Mary remembers a healthcare professional telling her, at one point, that life – both her own and her son's – was 'always going to look like this'. She remembers being horrified, especially that there was no hope being offered. Her distress was fuelled by the feelings of loneliness and shame that she experienced, particularly when she was in the waiting room of the Child and Adolescent Mental Health Service (CAMHS). Sometimes she felt unable to cope and in the depths of despair.

Her first decision was to join her local support group run by the Church, although she wasn't religious herself. For the first three months, it was only her, a friend and the kind lady who ran the support group. Mary recalls the first person who did arrive – a doctor who just couldn't face driving home to the family who awaited her. Eventually the group, based on the idea of parents helping each other in the midst of their own distress with the support of the Church, was the key to Mary coping with Bailey and all the challenges they faced. At first, it was run on a voluntary basis but, as numbers grew, the Church received some additional support.

Mary began to find better ways of supporting her son. One idea was to give Bailey a first-aid kit for 'harm minimisation' and show him how to use it. 'Obviously this was not an ideal situation to be in, but this was the reality of self-harming and I decided to work with my son to minimise the risks of the cutting that I just couldn't stop happening.' On another occasion, Mary recalls putting together a 'coping box' for her son which had ideas for how to manage at particularly stressful times. She says it was 'flatly rejected' but, on looking back, Mary thinks that it was good idea and might have worked if she had involved Bailey in putting it together rather than working on it alone.

As far as looking after her own mental health is concerned, Mary prioritises 'tea and cake with my friends, whenever possible'.

She also remembers the contribution of a friend who said that although she couldn't help Bailey, she could help Mary – and this was through teaching her some self-help techniques. The first, 'which might save my life', was how to 'take a single deep breath, hold it and breathe out properly'. Another was, for however brief a moment, to 'take a step outside myself and look in at the situation as if I was an outsider'.

What helped

- Attending a support group
- Having tea and cake with a particular person
- Creating a 'coping box'
- Some professional support and techniques from the internet

Rita

Rita is middle-aged, with a daughter, son-in-law and their baby living in the USA and a thirty-year-old son living at home. She was widowed relatively young but, after a few years, she started to find contentment rather than misery in living alone. Her son came back to the family home a few years ago. He suffers periodically with depression.

At first Rita was embarrassed and ashamed to find that she resented her son's return. She had started to get constructively involved with the cultural and social life of her local community. It was difficult for her to deal with her son's misery and sense of exclusion. He wants to be independent but often feels frustrated and behaves irresponsibly and without consideration.

Rita credits a good neighbour – who became a good friend – with helping her to step beyond the stifling resentment. The two of them shared a love of cookery so, after much swapping of ideas, they decided to collaborate in supplying traditional food for a couple of local businesses. They now make a modest profit and, more importantly, their collaboration encourages creativity as they swap ideas and experiment with new dishes. Rita has found this very empowering.

Privately, Rita has returned to an interest which she had more or less abandoned during the time of her marriage. She has taken up painting and enjoys the peacefulness of this hobby. It has also led to a further sense of creativity: she has taken a course in illustration, which might lead somewhere, and is thinking of displaying her work in Arts Week at some future date.

Although Rita feels rather helpless in the face of her son's depression, she feels that trying to be outgoing, productive and entrepreneurial are all life-changers.

What helped

- Joining a community project
- Developing a forgotten talent
- Building on a productive friendship

Ann

Ann has been married to Adam (see below) for forty years. Ann is now sixty-five. She gave up her work as a teacher to support her children with their substantial psychological issues.

Ann and Adam's older child, Kat, struggled increasingly from early adolescence and finally dropped out of school at fourteen. She developed acute psychosis in her early twenties, underwent several prolonged hospital admissions and died by suicide at twenty-five, while in a psychiatric ward. Their son Fred also has severe, ongoing mental health issues.

At the time we spoke, it was seven years since Kat had died. Ann discussed the shock of Kat and Fred developing mental health difficulties, when they had been happy children and had had a loving and supportive upbringing. She said she had to learn, slowly, how to live with the gradual loss of the healthy, cheerful lives the children deserved and 'should' have enjoyed. Then, since Kat's death, she has had to work on another level of grief to find continuing meaning in her life. 'I needed to keep on being a person who wasn't just a mother of an ill child.'

Ann has found becoming immersed in something – walking, writing, listening to and playing music, practising yoga – has helped at times. Walking and writing have enabled her to dive deeper into her situation and find the words and ideas to express it, so she can regard it with more clarity. Yoga, a constant in her life for many years, that she had thought would never let her down, became inaccessible for a time. This may have been because it was when she was in her little yoga room that the police came to tell her and Adam about Kat's suicide. Gradually, though, she became able to practise again, though it was a long time before she could use the same room.

Music has helped Ann too. In the early days, playing the cello – especially practising a piece she struggled with – helped and she could get lost in that. And she got obsessive about a choir she was in, saying it 'took her out of herself'. Choir practices were a slice of normality, where almost no one knew what had happened. Ann was treated as the same person as before, even when she went two days after Kat died, and that felt important to her. After a while, however, she couldn't do it anymore and she says she will never do it again. Emotions that bubbled up through singing became too much as the numbness wore off. Ann then replaced choir with a botany course, where she told no one about Kat. She loves the continuity and repeating cycles and resilience she sees in nature, particularly in looking at a tree and seeing it in all its aspects. 'It reminds me of being a child.'

Ann has found it useful to find ways to help other people, on a number of levels, from cleaning things for people ('a little corner I've made better') to joining an activist group trying to preserve green space for local people whose access to it is threatened. The effort she has had to make to learn about legislation and making formal objections, standing up for community rights, has absorbed her at times and helped her feel part of society, instead of an exception – someone whose child died before she did.

Ann says she has felt grief and the loss of the lives both her children might have lived, and her efforts to support Fred continue while she tries to comprehend what happened to Kat.

'Grief is remaking the destroyed parts of yourself. Every surface that comes into contact with any kind of thought about the child. Those surfaces eroded and destroyed. You lose your skin, so you feel raw. Everything you do involves remaking your inner and outer surfaces, so that you can function. On a practical level, sometimes you can't do normal things thoughtlessly. A mug, a drawing on a scrap of paper, a cushion, a hoodie – countless things contain an imprint of my child's life when she was here, and I have to tread so carefully. And there are always things that catch you unawares. Guilt is one of those. Everyone knows about guilt in grief, but it can rear up in a second. It's a mish-mash of emotions and selective memory. It helps to have someone to remind you of all the ways you've been the best parent you could be. Failing that, I try to look at it carefully, trace it back to what triggered it and why. Have a good cry, do some small, useful thing. I've learnt that I have to take the time I have to take to do all this.'

And it isn't always relentless. 'Some days, it feels like I'm skating on thin ice, and the grief work's going on underneath, like leaving the washing machine going, and then you hang it out, and it's done. But it might get you again when you fold it up. You can have several days like that, a bit of respite when you seem to be managing, and then you feel really bad about having been comparatively OK. Gradually though, I can pick out more moments I think about Kat, but they don't hook and hurt me so sharply. She's there, keeping me company, always liable to be round a corner, and we chat a bit, especially in the car, and she'll make fun of me. Just the same. I suppose those days get more while the work goes on, like healing a cut. A parent I met whose teenager died twenty years ago told me she has times when she is aware of being very happy, "not ecstatic, but really happy". I know what she meant. You never lose touch with what has happened, you're never the same, but you can change and grow into it, and that's how grief works.

'I have scars on my arms that Kat made, when she was psychotic. I absolutely love those cuts. There's one on each arm that show specially when I get a bit of a tan. When I want to reassure myself, I look at those. But actually, I have them everywhere, inside and out. All over, I'm at different stages of scarring. That'll go on and it's an essential part of me because I'll always be Kat's mum. Part of that, for me, is sometimes doing things to prove I'm still here and still myself – for me as well as for my whole family, including Kat.'

What helped

- Do things – whatever appeals to you – to make you feel more yourself
- Give grief time. Don't impose limits or goals or deadlines to achieve

- Stay open to possibilities and opportunities – especially shared projects
- Notice when happiness creeps in. Don't let guilt spoil it

Adam

Adam is married to Ann (see above) and is also sixty-five. He is a computer scientist, and has taught in further education, but has now retired. Adam is the father of Kat and Fred.

Adam spoke about having focused a lot on the practical things he could do to help, and the many things he and Ann had tried over the years to make their children's lives easier. He also spoke about loss, and about the constant change in the world.

Adam said 'I do best at a technical level – getting the resources required. I get Fred's car fixed. You're always ducking and diving with your child, you've got to keep flexibility. You have to play it day by day. Strategy is based on hindsight – what you're really aware of is day-to-day survival: I do see extreme value in keeping other people happy. I do really try at that. With food, walks, dogs and so on.'

Adam spoke more tangentially than Ann did about grief. 'A shared sense of humour with your kids definitely helps. I had that a lot with Kat. I miss Kat hugely. She was so very much herself. Always. We just understood each other. Life's not so much fun without her and I miss that fun, and having a laugh with her, even – especially – about serious stuff. She asked very serious questions and I miss that too. It doesn't always make me despair – she's gone away from here but she's still Kat somewhere. I'm deeply sad she's not here with us now.'

Adam worries about the difficulties of getting older, especially when you have children who are struggling. 'Ageing is very poignant when leaving behind a disabled child. It emphasises your ageing. With diminishing capabilities yourself, you can help less.'

He also spoke about the importance of being able to shift perspective and how it is crucial in his ability to cope. 'As a parent you can get tunnel vision, totally focused on offspring. Cocooning them in a negative way.' He also thinks it helps to see the world as something greater than we can conceive: 'I try and see a bigger universe with more opportunity. Every model, every way of thinking has limitations.'

What helped

- Accept that you can grieve in your own way
- Tackle jobs that fit your particular abilities
- Cherish your own, individual experience of the child who has died
- Recognise your strengths and work on them

Adam and Ann both mentioned relying on and still loving each other profoundly, but that this has sometimes been extremely difficult and that they've had to learn to live with differences in how they have coped over the years.

Ann: 'I'll show him something/point something out to him. Something that's completely wrecked me – like a drawing Kat did. And he'll say, "Ah yes, happy days". And I'll think, "WHAT?!" I usually don't say anything, although sometimes something like, "Well, it doesn't make me feel happy".

'Adam suffers in different ways. In some ways, he's just not quite so obsessed as me. Quite often, in every single box I open, every single thing will be something that hooks me and hurts. And I don't think he has any conception of what that's like. The physicality of it. I'll look at my hand, and remember how different Kat's were, and what they felt like. Every time I look at my feet, I remember massaging Kat's feet. I don't think he does it at all.'

Both Adam and Ann spoke about how they've been able to have a laugh sometimes, even when things were at their worst. They re-watch TV shows they found funny years ago, and there are many things both their kids have said and done which still make them laugh. 'Having jokes together was a big part of our relationship right from when we were young. Even when things are very dark, I know that at some point, we can get back to that.'

What helped

- Recognise that your ways are not other people's ways. Respect the differences
- Be flexible when possible and realise that other people have sticking points too
- Let your emotions show when possible and accept that other people may not be able to

SECTION 1:
OVERVIEW SUMMARY AND KEY MESSAGES

The stories that people shared with us were all different. No two journeys were the same. There was no clear winner in terms of a way to cope. What was consistent was that everyone had, somehow or other, managed to find their way through. It took longer for some than others. Finding the right support network and being able to look at things from different perspectives, were key parts of helping to manage and so was remembering that looking after oneself – even just a little – is critical to keeping on going. Below, we have drawn out some common themes that emerged from people's very varied, personal experiences and can be broadly divided into internal and external strategies.

Internal	External
Getting knowledge as part of problem-solving	Connecting with others – friends, professionals and the internet
Trying to think differently about the situation	Doing things for me such as engaging in hobbies
Accepting help	Getting a break
Deciding on priorities	Helping other people
Keeping a sense of humour	
Acceptance	

The next sections of the book describe some of these strategies in more detail, drawing on both people's personal experiences and psychological research about what can help.

SECTION 2:
UNTANGLING YOURSELF
FROM YOUR CHILD

2: Untangling yourself from your child: Why and how

Importance of untangling

Many of us believe that our children's needs come before our own. We *chose* to have children; they are helpless, so their needs should be prioritised. This belief is not universally shared (just do a quick google search of 'why your children don't come first'), and it wasn't always the case. The expression 'children should be seen and not heard', popularised in Victorian times, reflects their status as having fewer rights than adults. But today we tend to prioritise our children's needs and sacrifice our own in the process. For much of the time, that's a choice that we make in terms of doing without material possessions so that our money is spent on the children instead; we often don't manage to get in the exercise we would like and most of us certainly don't have the social life or fun that we used to have before children. Our lives and our children's lives get intertwined and when our children are unhappy, it is hard not to continue with the same pattern of doing everything we can for them and putting our needs (and those of our partners) bottom of the list.

But, as described in Chapter 1, that can be doubly unhelpful, which is why we thought that writing a book to help parents cope when their child can't might be useful. A key part of managing and coping is to remember that you are not your child and to try to keep a degree of healthy separation between helping and supporting your child as a parent and being completely consumed by your child's needs.

You are not alone: Becky's story

Becky is the mum of two boys and a girl; all have refused school due to anxiety. She worked in administration prior to the children but, due to the challenges of being a mum of three children with special needs, gradually reduced her hours. She tried working for just a day a week but even that became too much as she was constantly being called by school to collect one of the children, or to come in to discuss an issue. She also found it difficult to get to work on time on that single day she was meant to be working as one of the children would refuse to go to school and couldn't be left with anyone since her husband earned more money than Becky, so his work was prioritised over hers. She viewed being a mum as her job and one that she wanted to excel in. However, the daily stress of being a mum to her children, and also realising that they had inherited or learned some of their difficulties from her, led her to feel a failure as a parent.

> *'Being a good mum was, and is, so important to me. But I was failing. Failing to get them to school. Failing in helping them make friends. Failing to help them to be happy and get on in the world. I just wanted to walk out but I knew that I couldn't. I also knew that I had to get some help for myself. Eventually I went to the GP and got some tablets for my own depression and also went to see a counsellor. It took a long time, but I gradually realised that I needed to create some distance between me and my kids. I learned to appreciate what I was doing well, and what I wasn't. What really helped in the end was getting some time for myself to*

> *think things through and talk things through. Realising that*
> *I couldn't change them (however hard I want to try) – if*
> *they are not able or prepared to change – took time but*
> *was ultimately a massive relief. It wasn't going to happen,*
> *and I had to let that go.'*

Over-involvement

Some psychologists use the rather unpleasant and judgemental word 'enmeshment' to describe a blurring of boundaries between people, most commonly within families. It comes from the developers of family therapy in the 1970s and means that a parent focuses too much of their actions or too many emotions on the children. While caring and love within families is desirable and beneficial, there is recognition that a parent can be over-involved in their child's life, or at least some aspects of it and at some stages. Examples from family therapy include a lack of appropriate privacy between the parent and child or a parent being overly invested in their child's activities and achievement.

There is a downside to this for both the parent and the child. For the child, they often feel that they have to take care of the parent, that they can't confide in the parent because the parent will become upset and distressed and/or take over or interfere. The child may not develop his or her own individual sense of identity, worthiness or confidence in tackling new challenges which can have a knock-on effect on self-esteem. Sometimes the child may feel controlled and increasingly angry and resentful towards their parent, or alternatively withdraw completely. Over-involvement of parents can impact on relationships with peers, partners and also set up unrealistic expectations for future relationships. On a TV dating show,

43

one person on a date brought their mum along . . . Unsurprisingly, this put people off having a second date with them!

For the parent, knowing every detail of your child's life can fuel the fire of worry and questions ('Peter didn't wait for you when going into lunch? Are you being left out? Is he bullying you? Do you have other friends? What did you do first that meant he didn't wait?'). It can also lead to a very strong and pervasive sense of guilt about spending any time away from your child (see Chapter 11). What emerges is a strong pressure to be close to home at all times and to spend every minute with the family rather than pursuing your own interests.

Nobody knows what it is like to be you

When a child is unhappy, in pain or vulnerable due to a variety of possible reasons, the risk and consequences of 'enmeshment' are greater than when a child is bouncing along taking life in his/her stride. It may also be the case that what seems like unhelpful 'enmeshment' for a family with a child who takes life in their stride, is actually helpful, supportive and caring parenting in a child with a special need such as autism. This brings us to a major theme in the book that will be repeated throughout:

KEY POINT

Each one of us is different. Our families are unique. Our personalities are individual. There is no 'one size fits all' approach to trying to best get through the difficulties of parenting and to try to maintain your own mental and physical health in the face of your children's unhappiness.

You are not alone: Connie's story

Connie is in her early sixties. She told us her daughter's story.

'Winifred was always larger than the other girls. I am large, my mum was large, and so was Winnie. The internet was really just getting going when Winnie was a teenager, and it was a bad time to be overweight. There wasn't as much awareness of cyberbullying as there is now. Winnie would try to fit in with the other girls and post a picture – not in a bikini or anything, but maybe of a cute animal. She would get terrible comments about her size, her personality, anything. When she posted a picture of a ginger cat, she got comments about how boys would even prefer "gingers" to her . . . that type of thing. It really ground her down. I saw every post and every comment as she let me follow her. Every comment broke my heart. I cried more than her, I think. And Winnie saw my reaction. And she wanted me to stop following her so I didn't know, but that would have been worse. I needed to know. But knowing caused me such distress and looking back I don't know if it was helpful that I knew what was going on, or unhelpful because Winnie could see how upset it made me. Of course, nothing lasts forever. Children grow up and change and, although we never stop feeling responsible, as adults they might somehow make their own way and subsequently need us less. That is a callous thing to say, but being so involved and needed all the time was exhausting and it dominated my life. I would say it made me depressed and less able to help Winnie at the time she really needed me.'

Untangling yourself from your child

Untangling yourself from your child is likely to be in everyone's interests at times. Potential benefits are below:

For your child

- Less guilt/responsibility for you and your wellbeing
- More privacy
- More opportunities to try things for themselves
- Growing independence which builds confidence
- Learning to self-soothe
- Development of own identity
- Watch a model of a healthy adult–child relationship

For you

- More stable emotions
- Time! That time can be spent on hobbies for enjoyment, activities such as exercise or chores or . . . nothing
- Space to reflect on what is happening
- Space to be able to plan ahead for difficult situations before they escalate
- Ability to focus on needs of others in family (partner, other children)
- Development of other relationships including with parents in same position
- Less guilt when being away because you know it is in everyone's best interests

A key strategy for untangling yourself is to set some boundaries.

Untangling techniques

Setting boundaries is not for everyone. Feel free to skip this section if you know it is not for you. It may be you have tried setting limits for yourself and found it to be helpful. It may be the opposite – that you have found setting boundaries has caused more problems than it solved; e.g., by resulting in your child becoming more unhappy or angry.

Some people have strict boundaries, others have more flexible boundaries.

Boundaries are not rules for your child. Boundaries are rules for you – to protect you. In the same way, boundaries are not related to disciplining your child. Boundaries are within your control. Boundaries are about saying what is acceptable to you as a parent. Most people will have some boundaries – for example, that you will not get up after going to bed to make food for your child. What is key is to ensure that your child (and other family members) know your boundaries and these are clearly set out before a major incident. In order to do that, you need to be able to have the confidence to work out your boundaries and accept the consequences (e.g., your child having a meltdown). And you need to give yourself permission to accept that your boundaries may not be the same as other people's but as long as they work for you, then that's all matters.

Sharon Martin's blog on PsychCentral has some helpful ten step suggestions for creating boundaries (https://blogs.psychcentral.com/imperfect/2016/05/10-steps-to-setting-healthy-boundaries/). These steps are listed on the following pages.

1) Clearly identify your boundary. In keeping with the idea that there is no one approach that will work for everyone, we will all have different boundaries that are acceptable to each of us. It is very personal and depends so much on individual circumstances. Finding a boundary that you can manage and works for you and the family can be difficult, but the key principle is that it is designed to be helpful for you and to disentangle yourself from your child. Examples of such boundaries might include:

- I will not have my phone on so will not respond to texts or calls from you between 9–12.30 and 2–5 when I am working
- I will go for a run between 7.30 and 8.30am on Saturday, so will not be available then
- I will see my Mum on Wednesday nights so can't take you anywhere (your friends can come to us)
- I will go to bed at 11pm and can't help after that
- The kitchen is closed at 10pm so I won't be making food or fetching food after that time
- If you swear/yell/call me names, I will ignore you; I will only respond if you talk properly to me

You are not alone: Anoushri's story

Anoushri is a mother of two children, one of whom, Nikita, has a large birthmark on her face which makes her very self-conscious. Nikita first became aware that she was different when she went to primary school and a child told her that she had spilled paint on her face.

Anoushri had been concerned about what the children might say but she and her husband didn't want to put Nikita through the pain of plastic surgery and wanted to wait until she was older and could make her own decision. Over the years, Nikita became increasingly self-conscious about her appearance and wanted plastic surgery. Unfortunately, there was a medical complication which meant that her birthmark could not be removed. Nikita was devasted and blamed her mother (unreasonably) for not taking her to the doctor to have it removed at birth. She repeatedly told her mother that she had ruined her life, and Nikita refused to engage in social media or to go out anywhere other than school. When she went to secondary school, she began to use her mum's credit card without permission to buy a range of expensive products over the internet that promised to mask the birthmark or remove it. Anoushri put the following boundaries in place with Nikita and, importantly, they were discussed calmly, at the kitchen table, before another incident had taken place rather than being put in place in the middle of a major argument.

- I am going to change the password on my credit card and will not tell you it

- I will give you a limit of £25 per month to be spent on creams relating to birthmarks

- I will only answer questions seeking reassurance about the birthmark one time, and then I will say 'I have answered that question already and I don't think it is helpful to have the same discussion again'

2) Understand why you need the boundary. Even though you are only near the beginning of the book, we hope that it is clear why boundaries can be helpful to you and your child. Boundaries can help your child grow independently in confidence and discover what they cannot do.

You are not alone: Fatima's story

'I was just becoming exhausted from staying up, chatting to my son. I was having about five hours sleep a night and it made me ill, physically and mentally. I told him that I couldn't stay with him past midnight. He understood, although the first few days were difficult as I could hear him lying awake crying. After a few nights, it settled down and I just felt much better for having some sleep and much more able to cope with the challenges that lay ahead.'

---

3) Be straightforward. It's easy to get complicated. It's hard to be simple. But stating the boundary really clearly, writing it down, drawing it, sticking it on the fridge, sending it in a text, all done in a calm manner before a major blow-up, is key to successfully being able to follow it. There are some key principles of communication with your child that can help:

- Make good eye contact as you are stating the boundary to make sure you have your child's attention
- Reduce distractions
- Try not to have an audience (siblings) around unless the boundary applies to them too
- Try to ensure consistency so that you are not doing one thing for one child and another for a different child
- Be clear about when this will start – e.g., from tonight/tomorrow . . .
- Ask your child to repeat the boundary back to you so you know they have understood

4) Don't apologise or give long explanations. For Anoushri, she could easily have said to Nikita that she was sorry that she couldn't afford more than £25 per month on products. But this would have given the message that £25 isn't enough whereas in reality, there was no magic potion that would help with her skin condition. Similarly, it is not unreasonable to make a division between home and work, or to prioritise your sleep or exercise, without an apology or long explanation.

5) Use a calm and polite tone. Part of setting boundaries is the 'modelling' of behaviour that we want to see. Being yelled at and sworn at by our children (some will be shocked that this is tolerated, others will know it's just a way of life) is not desirable and it's tempting to swear back. Our behaviour undoubtedly gives important messages to our children, so we need boundaries to give ourselves the ability and resources to stay calm. It's challenging to stay calm when stressed – when the demands on us are greater than our ability to meet them. But walking away so that we can stay calm, gather our thoughts and return calmly is truly in everyone's best interests.

6) Start with tighter boundaries then loosen if appropriate – SMART boundaries. This is tricky. What is reasonable? What is not? Asking others where they have set the boundaries can be helpful information when deciding where to set yours, but bear in mind the principle that everyone is different. There's some trial and error in boundary setting but it may be worth borrowing some of the ideas from the setting of goals, and those goals should be 'SMART':

- Specific
- Measurable

- Achievable
- Relevant
- Time-bound

Applying this to boundary-setting may be helpful. Some examples are below.

- Specific – I will not be available before 7am so that I have time to shower and get dressed to start the day
- Measurable – Are you showered and dressed before 7am?
- Achievable – Is it achievable or does your child typically want you most at that time? How many days have you managed this in the last month? If none, then it may be that it's too challenging at this time.
- Relevant – Would it make a difference to your day if you knew you had this time every morning and started the day off being showered and dressed?
- Time-bound – How long are you going to try this for? Is it easier to start with it for one week and then relax/change the boundary depending on how things have gone? You may want to tell your child that you are trying this boundary for a week and then will have a discussion about how it has gone.

7) Address boundary violations early and praise when boundaries are kept. There is a lot going on in all of our lives. It can be easy to set too many boundaries or too strict boundaries all in one go, but simpler is better so that boundaries can be prioritised, and difficulties addressed early on. The key to setting boundaries is to ensure that they are within your control. But what if they are violated so, for example, Nikita found out Anoushri's new password and used her credit card without permission? If that happens, it needs to be clear what the consequences are, and it is really important to follow through on those for future boundary setting. Although it can feel harsh, it helps to remember that boundaries help your child as well as you. It's even better to try to prevent boundary violations from happening by using common parenting strategies such as praise for keeping to boundaries (praise for yourself as well as your child!). Praise can be forgotten in the middle of the storm of unhappiness, but the following principles are worth remembering when praising:

- Offer immediate praise – It's great you kept to the agreement of not coming in before 7am this morning. Well done!
- Offer consistent praise – Use your positive attention for every boundary that is followed
- Offer specific praise – You got yourself food rather than bothering me as you know that I have said I won't get food after 10pm. That's fantastic. Well done!
- Ensure you have your child's attention in the same way as when you were setting the boundary

8) Don't make it personal. It is easy to comment on how draining you find your child compared perhaps to another of your children, or to other people's children. It's important to try to be clear that setting the boundary isn't a criticism of your child or a failure on your part to be able to give enough time or energy. If you say, 'I will not be available before 7am', your child may hear 'I'm a bother, my mum can't face seeing me first thing'. So being very clear about the reasons you are setting the boundaries without an apology or long explanation is helpful (see point 4).

9) Use a support system. It was clear from the stories in Section 1 that a support system is essential. A support system does more than just support – it offers insight into what other people do in challenging situations and what is 'normal'. Although 'normal' may not apply to you (we haven't met any people who it does apply to), it can be a helpful context. For example, the question of how much help to give your child with schoolwork is an interesting one. Some families are of the view that no help is best so that the school know what is going on and can provide appropriate support. Others consider that they want to give their child every possible support so they don't get behind. It's back to there not being a 'one size fits all' principle and each of us has our own value system and makes the decisions we feel are best for our personal circumstance. Making that decision though is best done from an informed position and so talking to others about what they do can be helpful. It can also give us permission to not help at times without feeling guilty.

10) Trust your gut. Nobody knows your family like you do. It's impossible to explain to professionals what living with an unhappy child is like. Simple suggestions can trigger intense feelings of anger because, let's face it, we're not stupid. We know the basic idea of parenting and, truth be told, this is unlikely to be the first self-help book you have bought (although if it is, then that's great) and we have a list of other useful books and helpful websites at the end of this one in the 'Further resources' section. So, we know the ideas, we try to put them into practice. It doesn't always work.

Exercise 2.1: Establishing boundaries

Think of a boundary that you would like to put in place . . .

. . . .

What would be the advantages of having this boundary?

For you . . .

. . . .

For your child . . .

. . . .

For anyone else in the family (e.g., sibling) . . .

. . . .

Is this boundary SMART (Specific, Measurable, Achievable, Relevant, Time-bound)?

If Yes . . . Carry on. If No . . . Rethink the boundary so it is SMART . . .

When do you plan to discuss the boundary?

. . . .

How will you make sure it is done in a calm way, with no distractions, etc.?

. . . .

How will you handle any arguments about the boundary?

. . . .

Put the Boundary in Place for one week

Reflection: What happened?

What boundary did you actually put in place?

....

How did the discussion about the boundary go? Would you do anything differently next time?

....

What were the consequences of having the boundary in place?

Positive for you ....

Negative for you ....

Positive for your child ....

Negative for your child ....

Positive for others ....

Negative for others ....

Conclusion: Is boundary setting a helpful technique for you? YES/NO

Boundaries vs. punishment

Household rules, and consequences of those, are not the same as personal boundaries that you put in place to separate yourself from your child. This is a very important distinction. The issue of punishment and discipline is challenging but it certainly seems as though for some people, parental 'warmth' can be a better way forward. Yet it seems wrong as parents not to 'teach' our children the best way to behave. Separating 'punishment' from 'consequences of behaviour' can be helpful, and viewing your attention as a way to provide reward for good behaviour while ignoring behaviour you want reduced can be a helpful parenting tool (see Further resources for more on this).

You are not alone: Michele's story

'Punishment never seemed to work for my son, Jon. He was eight when he articulated it. "You punishing me just makes me more angry because it's so unfair. I feel I have nothing left to lose. So, I may as well lose everything right now.". I remember when he texted me a photo of the self-help book I had bought about how to help manage his behaviour. I had bought it after he had texted me a photo while I was at work of him trashing his older brother's new expensive trainers. He was trying to get my attention because I had told him that I would not be responding to messages while at work. That was the boundary that I needed to set for my own sanity, not to mention work. The book was ripped up in his hands and covered in muck. He was smiling in the photo. The message was clear – I am going to win and there's nothing you can do about it. I felt utterly hopeless and agreed with him – he was going to win. Over lunch, my colleagues could tell I was upset so I told them what had happened. Their warmth and sympathy helped me see a funny side and we shared stories of the various setbacks we had had along the way with parenting. I felt better after lunch and more able to focus on my work and my day. I didn't respond to the photo as I had a boundary in place – I had told him that I wouldn't

---

be responding to messages and I didn't. I decided to just deal with it all when I got home and although it definitely affected my work, I did feel better that I had stuck to my boundaries and actually by the time I got home, both of us had calmed down.'

SECTION 2:
OVERVIEW SUMMARY AND KEY MESSAGES

- You are not your child

- Separating a bit from your child can be of benefit to you and also your child and family

- Strategies to set boundaries to help are suggested

- SMART boundaries will be most helpful

- Different boundaries will be needed for different children – there is no one size fits all

SECTION 3:
HELPFUL STRATEGIES

Introduction to Section 3

The term 'mental health science' is used more nowadays, but scientific experiments to understand how to help anxiety and behaviour have been going on for almost eighty years. One of the most famous early experiments from psychology research involved 'Little Albert', a baby who was shown various animals (including a rat) and objects. At the beginning, the baby wasn't afraid of the rat. He was, however, unsurprisingly upset by a loud noise that the scientists made, and he started to cry. The scientists showed Little Albert the rat together with the noise a few times and each time Albert was upset and cried. Finally, Little Albert would cry on just seeing the rat and the scientists had some information on how some children become anxious and upset. The next obvious step for the scientists was to begin to think about how best to reduce emotional distress. This led to lots of scientific studies of different methods and techniques to reduce anxiety. Those studies formed the basis of many of the effective psychological therapies that are still used today.

But what of Little Albert's mother? Decades after the scientific experiment, researchers found out that she had been paid for Little Albert to take part in the experiment but there is little about how she felt about watching Little Albert get upset. It's not known how long Little Albert's anxiety lasted, or whether she regretted him taking part. She did help pave the way for other scientific studies though and, as a result, scientists do have some good information on what psychological treatments can be helpful. They still often don't really know which particular parts of the psychological treatments are the most important. They are also working hard to find out what psychological treatments are best for different types of people because, as has been stated throughout the book, no two people are the same. We are all very different and have hugely varied experiences with our children.

Even though there is a lot more work to be done, we thought it was important to include some 'tried and tested' strategies from psychology research, and that's the focus of Section 3. In this section (Chapters 3 to 14), we give some ideas for possible strategies (all of which have a basis in scientific studies) to help you deal with the situation you are in. Some chapters might help you to deal with the practicalities of coping with the difficulties of being a parent to a child who's suffering. Others will help you to recognise and understand your own feelings, thoughts and behaviours in relation to the situation, and to try some techniques for thinking differently, feeling better and changing unhelpful behaviours. Together with the 'top tips' from other parents in Section 4, these strategies should help you cope when your child can't.

3: Problem-solving

One of the most important techniques is problem-solving. The reasons we like problem-solving are:

- It makes sense
- It is straightforward to understand
- It works. Science has shown it can be effective for depression and it is also used in effective treatments for other problems such as anxiety and perfectionism

What is problem-solving?

In some ways, problem-solving is exactly what its name suggests – it's a method to help solve problems. It does this by helping you go through a series of steps in a calm, objective way. Instead of the problems going round and round in your head, it helps break them down and separates them so that they are less overwhelming. It is a starting point for being able to change and to see the impact of that change.

When should it be used and when shouldn't it?

In one of the leading psychological treatments for anxiety developed by Canadian researchers, a distinction is made between worries that can be helped using problem-solving and those that cannot. Problem-solving won't help future hypothetical or 'what if' situations. Those are the things that you can't do anything about, so it's important to try to change your reaction to the situation rather than the situation itself. The situations that you can do something about that relate to current problems are where problem-solving is helpful. An example of a current problem that could be helped with problem-solving and an example of a hypothetical problem that cannot are shown below:

Hypothetical problem

Tolu was the mother of two children, aged five and thirteen. Her thirteen-year-old daughter was non-verbal and had severe intellectual disabilities. She was very dependent on her mum for everything. Only Tolu could comfort her daughter when she was distressed, and only she knew what her various sounds meant she wanted. Her five-year-old son had a severe nut allergy, and Tolu was always very careful about the content of food so that he would be safe. Tolu worried constantly about both of her children. One evening, Tolu noticed a lump in her breast and was immediately very frightened that she had breast cancer. She went to the doctor and later had a biopsy. While she was waiting for the results, she was very stressed and irritable with the children, which in turn made them very grumpy, so there was even more stress than usual in her house. The biopsy was thankfully negative, but Tolu had begun to notice a lot of other symptoms. She couldn't sleep at night for worrying about what would happen to the children if anything happened to her. She had a series of tests, all of which were negative, but that didn't help her as she worried that the doctors just hadn't found the problem, which might mean that it would be too late when they did. Tolu's worries spiralled out of control and the more worried she became, the more unhappy her children were – which made her feel that they needed her even more and so the worries about her health continued in a vicious cycle.

Tolu's worries wouldn't be helped with problem-solving because they are hypothetical, 'what-if' future worries. If you have these types of worries and they are interfering with your life, and affecting your family, then it would be worth getting some support for them from your GP or a talking therapy service (see Further resources). There are also some good self-help books you can read that help tolerate uncertainty such as the one by Melissa Robichaud and Michel Dugas (*The Generalized Anxiety Disorder Workbook*, 2016).

Current problem

Fatima's daughter Sienna (sixteen) had been the victim of bullying at school and cyberbullying a couple of years ago. Fatima hadn't known about it for a few months and felt very guilty about that. Once she knew, she did all that she could to help – she spoke to other parents, went to the school and she also had Sienna's passwords so she could keep an eye on what was going on. The bullying was better, but Fatima still checked Sienna's social media accounts daily, and got very upset if anything was posted that she thought could be considered negative about Sienna. She discussed the posts with Sienna, who was increasingly frustrated by her mum's behaviour and asked her to stop checking her accounts. Sienna tried to change the passwords, but Fatima got so upset that Sienna told her the new passwords. Fatima and Sienna often fought about what Sienna posted. Sienna told her mother to 'butt out' now and let Sienna handle the situations herself. Fatima knew that she should do this but was so worried about the bullying starting again and her desire to protect Sienna that she just couldn't stop checking Sienna's accounts, despite the arguments at home.

Fatima's worries would be helped with problem-solving because they are current, real problems that have a potential solution.

Below are two exercises to help you to see if problem-solving might be useful for you to try to remain positive even when your child is going through a tough time. The first is a quiz to help you identify what kinds of concerns can be helped by problem-solving. The concerns that can be helped by problem-solving are *current, practical, real-world issues* rather than 'what if' types of concerns. Cover up the columns to the right of the concern and see if you were right in the sort of problems that can be helped by problem-solving. The second exercise is to list your own concerns and see if they could be helped with problem-solving.

Exercise 3.1: What concerns can be helped by problem-solving?			
Concern	**Current, practical? (Y/N)**	**Helped by Problem-Solving (Y/N)**	**Comment**
1. You are exhausted from staying up with your child to help get him/her to bed at night.	Y	Y	Problem-solving will help find solutions to you being exhausted and come up with alternative strategies.

2. You are worried that your child will harm themselves.	Y	Y	Problem-solving can be helpful to some extent in terms of making sure you have taken all the steps you can to reduce the chance of harm.
3. You might become ill in the future.	N	N	This is a 'what if' future worry so problem-solving is unlikely to be that helpful.
4. Your child is friends with someone you think is a bad influence and likely to get them into trouble.	N	N	This is not something that is within your control – it's not a problem you can solve.
5. You can't sleep at night for worrying about your child's unhappiness.	Y	Y	Problem-solving will help you identify ways of managing your worries to help you sleep.

Exercise 3.2: Which of your concerns can be helped by problem-solving?			
Concern	**Is it current?**	**Is it practical?**	**Does it have a 'what if' part to it?**

If your concerns are current, practical and are *not* the 'what if' type of worries, then problem-solving might be helpful to you in trying to remain positive despite the challenges your child may be experiencing.

Steps to problem-solving

There are five recognised steps to problem-solving that can helpfully be remembered using the acronym 'I D E A L'. When doing these steps, it really does help to write things down, as getting it on paper helps you get some distance and clarifies your thinking. It can truly stop the whirring in your head:

I – Identify the problem – as early as possible

D – Define the problem – be as precise as possible; only one problem at a time

E – Explore the potential solutions by brainstorming without judgement

A – Action a solution; decide on one of the solutions

L – Learn from the action – what worked, what didn't

I – Identify the problem – as early as possible

This is (another) one of those things that is harder to do in reality than it sounds. When there is so much going on in your head, it can be really tricky to identify the problem as early as possible. Sometimes it is helpful to think about past experiences when you identified a problem late and think about what you learned from that. Take the example below:

You are not alone: Shoshana's story

Shoshana described how distressed her daughter, Mimi, was at leaving her when she first went to nursery at two years old. This was very different from the other new child who just waved his mum off and went in happily. Shoshana remembered feeling as though she had failed Mimi, and this was made worse by the nursery teacher asking her if anything was wrong at home. On the first day of school at four years old, Mimi was the only one that cried and had to be pulled off her mum. Shoshana remembered sobbing in the car, wondering what she was doing wrong, feeling guilty and thinking she was a terrible mother. Going to secondary school was also very stressful, with Mimi getting in trouble in the first term and hating every minute of it. Shoshana jumped every time the phone rang, thinking it was school with a terrible message about Mimi. When talking about it, Shoshana could see that she hadn't done anything wrong in raising Mimi, but Mimi reacted badly to these changes; she could also see that her own anxiety and fear/dislike of teachers was making her worry about Mimi at school even when that wasn't necessary. Shoshana used problem-solving to try to help her manage when Mimi was at school without constantly being terrified that the phone was going to ring with news about her daughter.

D – Define the problem – be as precise as possible; only one problem at a time

It is really important to remember that you are not trying to solve your child's unhappiness here. You can apply problem-solving very effectively to help solve *any* real, practical problem so that may include a problem with bullying, or accessing support, or helping your child become less sad. However, the focus of this book is on you. So, try to separate yourself from your child for the purposes of identifying the problem. *What is the problem for you?* Consider the examples below to help you identify the problem for you.

> *My child is unhappy: the problem for me is that I can't make him/her happy*

> *My child is unhappy: the problem for me is that I am so distressed about his/her unhappiness that I can't focus on work*

My child is unhappy: the problem for me is that I can't sleep at night for worrying

My child is unhappy: the problem for me is that he/she is taking up so much time with appointments, that I am neglecting the other children

My child is unhappy: the problem for me is that he/she is taking it out on me and yelling at me all the time

My child is unhappy: the problem for me is just that I hate to see her unhappy and it makes me unhappy too

E – Explore the potential solutions by brainstorming without judgement

This step involves brainstorming all possible solutions and thinking through the pros and cons of each. So, although it may be tempting to tell your child how unhappy they are making you in the hope that will change how they are feeling, there may be some important disadvantages of taking that path. An advantage might be that you would feel better in the short term, but in the longer term the disadvantage is that you might feel you are not being supportive, and your child is not able to tell you about their distress. A key to this step is to let your imagination run wild. 'Without judgement' is just that – anything goes in your imagination – however outrageous. Such 'out of the box' creative thinking is just the type of thinking that will allow you to come up with solutions that are harder to think of in the moment.

A – Action a solution; decide on one of the solutions

Working out the pros and cons of various solutions is challenging, but the next step is to decide, on balance, which solution you will action. Some actions might be incredibly difficult – for example deciding to call the police for your child, or agreeing to your child being sectioned. When you are feeling low yourself, such decisions are even more difficult to make and can be filled with a lot of guilt and self-doubt after the event. Deciding on one of the solutions on the basis of the pros and cons can be even more useful when you yourself are struggling with decision-making. One solution may have a stronger emotional pull than another, but seeing it on paper, with pros and cons written down, can really help you make a rational decision. It can also help with you being able to justify your decision at a later date – *I made the best decision that I could with the information that I had at the time.*

L – Learn from the action – what worked, what didn't

It would be wonderful if every decision we made about a course of action was the right one. Unfortunately, we often have to live with the uncertainty of not knowing if we made the right decision and the reality is that there usually isn't a right decision. That uncertainty is tough and being able to tolerate it and starting to accept it is a key part of being able to help manage emotions (see Further resources for books on how to help tolerate uncertainty; see Chapter 5 for some strategies on emotion regulation and Section 5 for some strategies to help with acceptance). Sometimes, sadly, we look back and realise it was the wrong decision or a bad outcome, despite the best of intentions. The best way forward then is to learn from that and try to use it when the next problem comes along. Often, though, the solution was a good one, and remembering what you did so that you can do it again is an important part of deciding what to do next time. Anything that helps you remember the decision and the outcome, such as writing it down in a notebook or on your phone, is likely to be helpful.

You are not alone: Sheetal's story

Rohail was a kind, fourteen-year-old boy who had always been quite shy. Recently, his mood had begun to get worse and he had started to refuse to go out of his room for anything other than school. This was causing a lot of problems for his parents as he had begun to refuse to come downstairs to greet his grandmother or go to family gatherings. His grandmother was furious and blamed his mother for being a weak parent unable to control her child. She would storm into his room and shout at him for being disrespectful. Later on, Rohail would shout at his mother, Sheetal, for allowing his grandmother to come into his room and make him feel worse than he already did. Sheetal was distressed by Rohail's behaviour and her mother's behaviour and didn't know what to do. On the advice of a friend, she tried problem-solving and her problem-solving worksheet is below.

I – Identify the problem – as early as possible

This problem has been there for about a month now so it's pretty early.

D – Define the problem – be as precise as possible; only one-problem at a time

I don't know if the problem is that Rohail is depressed, or disobedient, or if the problem is that I should control him better or that I should tell my mother to mind her own business and stop interfering. All of those are problems. If I had to pick one, I think the one that makes me feel worst is that I feel criticised and judged by my mother who doesn't understand the situation that I am dealing with.

E – Explore the potential solutions by brainstorming without judgement

(1) Tell my mother how her behaviour makes me feel.

PRO: that's what I know I *should* do. I might feel better if I was honest.

CON: she'd never understand and would say that is where Rohail gets it from and feelings don't matter – it's what you do that counts. It may make it worse.

(2) I could stop inviting my mother over, so she doesn't get a chance to criticise me.

PRO: tempting. I'd like to stop inviting her over. I'd feel a lot better in the short term.

CON: completely unrealistic. She'd come over anyway and it would make it worse. She'd tell everyone about how badly I treated her.

(3) I could lie and say he has a contagious disease.

PRO: tempting. Would sort the problem out as he could stay in his room without being bothered and she wouldn't be so critical.

CON: she'd find me out – I'd never get away with it and that would make it all worse.

(4) I could try to explain that Rohail is having a tough time, that he might be depressed, and we are trying to get him help.

PRO: it's the truth. She may be more empathic.

CON: it's a risk. She's a gossip and everyone would know and Rohail would feel like I was betraying his trust.

(5) I could just try to ignore her criticism – she doesn't know the situation.

PRO: least bad solution – it wouldn't make the situation worse; I am changing my reaction to her rather than her which is more do-able.

CON: I don't know that I can do it. I know I should, but I don't know if I can.

A – Action a solution; decide on one of the solutions

I'm going to lie. I will look up the symptoms and tell my mother that he's got something that means he's contagious.

L – Learn from the action – what worked, what didn't

Actually, it worked quite well. I didn't feel guilty. Rohail looked really grateful as he knows that I don't usually lie, and it gave us both the breathing space that we needed. Although it worked, I know it's only short term as chickenpox only lasts one to three weeks and it only worked because it is the holidays. I hope Rohail is feeling better soon though, so it won't be an issue in a few weeks.

Exercise 3.3: Having a go at solving your own problem

This exercise gives you a chance to solve one of your own problems. You can use the worksheet below, or there are others that are easy to download from the internet if you search for 'problem-solving worksheets'. The worksheets may give the steps different names but that doesn't matter – the idea behind them is the same.

I – Identify the problem – as early as possible

....

....

D – Define the problem – be as precise as possible; only one problem at a time

....

....

E – Explore the potential solutions by brainstorming without judgement

....

....

A – Action a solution; decide on one of the solutions

....

....

L – Learn from the action – what worked, what didn't

....

....

It should also be noted that although some problems are current and real problems, as desperate parents we often try any and all potential solutions to help our children. This can particularly be the case when trying to get our child support that we believe may be potentially helpful but is difficult to obtain. Having exhausted all possible solutions, it may be the case that at times, for some people, under particular circumstances, acceptance may be an alternative option (see Chapter 18).

CHAPTER 3: SUMMARY AND KEY MESSAGES

- This chapter described a step-by-step technique for helping to solve problems

- Before you even start, you need to work out if this problem is current and practical

- If it is, then we would suggest you try problem-solving

- It's one of those methods that is best done properly at the beginning, sitting down with pen and paper

- Problem-solving is a helpful strategy for trying to give you hope and help for how you can manage when your child is sad

- It's not easy but it is worth giving the IDEAL steps a go

- Remember to define one problem at a time, and to look back and see the impact of your problem-solving to help for the next one

4: Increasing awareness of emotions and their triggers

Parenting a child who is unhappy can test even the most patient of people, and many of us find that our own emotions can be overwhelming and unhelpful. It's frustrating when our child procrastinates or avoids rather than getting on and doing their homework or chores or whatever is asked of them. And it's easy for us to see that the consequences of that avoidance just make the situation worse and makes them *more* unhappy. Why won't they take our good advice? Why won't they stick to the timetable we have carefully gone through with them? Or leave their phones outside their rooms as carefully agreed? Why, instead of thanking us for our words of wisdom, do they blame us? Often we are told that it is good that our children feel safe enough to vent their frustrations and take it out on us at home. We have been told that it is positive that home is a safe place. 'If they can't do it at home, where can they do it?' is a question posed by well-meaning friends and relatives, trying to make us feel better about the hideous situation we find ourselves in, where it feels as though we are being used as a verbal (and sometimes physical) punchbag. It is also the case that we often make an effort to be strong for our children in front of them and hide our own worries for their future, our own hopelessness, and sob silently into our pillows at night.

You are not alone: Suranne's story

Suranne, thirty-four, is a single mum of three boys aged three, six and nine. The boys have different fathers and only the six-year-old's dad is involved in his life. Her nine-year-old son, Kai, had a lot of problems concentrating at school and was often in trouble and got very upset whenever his brother's Dad was due to come round and take his brother out. Kai would often throw objects and beat his fists against the walls until he damaged them or himself. During these times, Suranne would do everything she could to calm him down at first, but Kai just couldn't or wouldn't listen. After about 10–15 minutes of trying to calm Kai down, Suranne would lose her temper. She usually ended up yelling at Kai and the three-year-old would then get upset too. It was completely overwhelming and Suranne would be exhausted by the end of the episode and usually everyone would end up crying. Suranne would also have the mess to clear up. The number of times this was happening was increasing and it was happening at times when Kai got upset about other situations too. Suranne sometimes felt that she was raising a monster who, she feared, was headed for a life of violent crime.

Can you learn to understand your emotions better and be more patient? Can having more patience help you deal with the daily stresses that accompany supporting your children and help you try to keep your own spirits up so you can support your other children, do your jobs, sort out the washing, cook and, possibly, even have some pleasure in life despite the situation?

Yes.

An interesting study by Sarah Schnitker involved developing a measure of patience and some strategies to help. The strategies were given over a two-week period which is not too long for those of us that don't have much time. They found the strategies improve patience and positive mood. These strategies were based on some broader ideas from positive psychology and clinical psychology, and involved:

1. increasing awareness of emotions and their triggers

2. emotion regulation strategies

3. techniques to help with stress in relation to others, and

4. developing empathy and compassion

These techniques (and some others from psychological research) are described in this chapter and the following chapters. There was also some guided meditation (see Further resources). The rest of this chapter has some techniques to help you with the first steps: to develop patience and stay emotionally well even when your child is not.

Increasing awareness of emotions and their triggers

Trying to understand emotions has kept psychologists in business for many years. Identifying emotions and their triggers is the first step to changing them. One of the most helpful ways to identify and understand emotions and their triggers is by thinking of the emotion and what it is usually associated with. The box below shows some common themes behind particular emotions.

Emotion	Associated with	Example
Anxiety	Threat	The threat of not being able to cope will lead to a feeling of anxiety and worry about the future
Sadness	Loss	The loss of normal social interactions, and loss of having the 'perfect' family will lead to feelings of sadness
Anger	Injustice/ unfairness	Thinking that something is unfair is associated with a sense of anger at the situation or person causing the injustice
Guilt	Breaking of moral standards	Having to lie to friends about why you can't meet up can make you feel guilty if you are not someone that usually lies

Identifying and understanding emotions can make them seem more predictable and controllable. In turn, this means that the strong, intense emotions will no longer take you by surprise, which should help make them less overwhelming. In the case of Suranne, she felt anger when Kai was upset and lost his temper because he was taking his anger out on her, wrecking his room, causing extra work for her, not listening to her and not calming down. Although rationally Suranne understood Kai's own anger, due to the unfairness of him not having his Dad around, it wasn't Suranne's fault and there was nothing she could do about the situation.

Some people find a 'Feelings Wheel' helpful in trying to identify their emotions. There are various versions of this wheel, but the one below was developed by Geoffrey Roberts and built on work by Kaitlin Robb and Gloria Willcox.

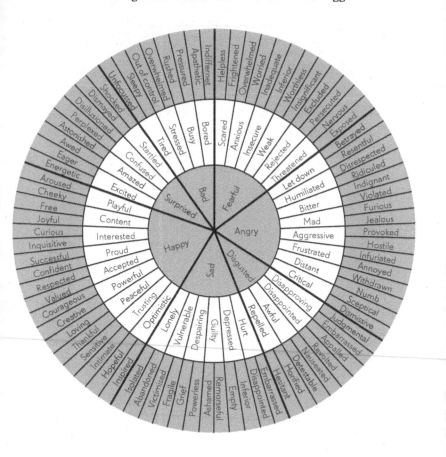

Exercise 4.1: Personal examples to associate the
emotion with the theme behind it

Think back to the last time you experienced each of the
emotions and fill in your own example:

Emotion	Associated with	Your own example
Anxiety	Threat	
Sadness	Loss	
Anger	Injustice/ unfairness	
Guilt	Breaking of moral standards	

OK, all well and good that you have identified the emotion.
Identifying your emotions in real-time can be particularly helpful,
so take a photo of the wheel with your phone so you can easily have
it to hand. Now what? The next chapters provide ways of managing
the emotions.

CHAPTER 4: SUMMARY AND KEY MESSAGES

- Our own emotions can be overwhelming and unhelpful at times

- Identifying our own emotions can help increase our patience and ability to cope

- Certain themes are associated with certain emotions e.g., anxiety is associated with threat

5: Emotion regulation strategies

Emotion regulation strategies

The examples in Chapter 15 on 'Small pleasures' are personal examples of how people try to regulate their emotions. What works for one person (like a cold swim in a lake) will not work for another. Much of the scientific research on emotion regulation comes from 'Dialectical Behaviour Therapy' and there are many helpful strategies you can find on the internet (e.g., https://positivepsychology. com/emotion-regulation-worksheets-strategies-dbt-skills/).

The fantastic 'getselfhelp' website uses a STOPP method to help you regulate your emotions in the moment when everything is kicking off. These emotions may be anxiety, anger or sadness, but they may also be the feelings of guilt, shame and jealousy (see Chapters 11, 12 and 14). Feeling 'upset', 'hopeless' or 'in despair' may best capture the mixture of emotions you feel at any point. If this describes you, then the 'STOPP' technique from cognitive behavioural therapy may help and give you hope that although you can't change the situation you find yourself in, you can change how you feel about the situation.

www.getselfhelp.co.uk/stopp/

5: Emotion regulation strategies

S – Stop!

* Wait a minute . . . (singing in the style of *Uptown Funk* can help make this memorable!)

T – Take a Breath

* Notice your breathing as you breathe in and out

O – Observe

* What thoughts are going through your mind right now?
* Where is your focus of attention?
* What are you reacting to? Is it the sense of unfairness? Loss? Threat?
* What sensations do you notice in your body?

P – Pull Back – Put in Some Perspective

* What's the bigger picture?
* Take the helicopter view
* What is another way of looking at this situation?
* What would a trusted friend say to me right now?
* Is this thought a fact or an opinion?
* What is a more reasonable explanation?
* How important is this? How important will it be in six months' time?

P – Practise What Works – Proceed

* What is the best thing to do right now? For me? For others? For the situation?
* What can I do that fits with my values?
* Do what will be effective and appropriate

For Suranne, her STOPP looked like this:

S – Stop!

- Wait a minute

T – Take a Breath

- Take three deep breaths (no time for more)

O – Observe

- What thoughts are going through your mind right now?

  Oh no, not again. I can't bear it. I know how it's going to end. F***ing H*ll.

- Where is your focus of attention?

  On the mess of his room, on the nightmare situation that I am in.

- What are you reacting to? Is it the sense of unfairness? Loss? Threat?

  I am reacting to my lack of control over the situation and my inability to calm Kai down (again).

- What sensations do you notice in your body?

  My heart is racing, my head is pounding. I feel such a surge of complete anger. Red anger.

P – Pull Back – Put in Some Perspective

- What's the bigger picture?

  Kai is nine years old. If I can't cope with my emotions, how can I expect him to?

5: Emotion regulation strategies

- Take the helicopter view

  I can see I am not helping but I can't help it.

- What is another way of looking at this situation?

  Kai is upset and is telling me that in the only way he can.

- What would a trusted friend say to me right now?

  Poor Suranne. Stay calm. Don't fuel it by responding. Just STAY CALM. It will be over quicker if you just ignore it but stay in the room to make sure he is safe.

- Is this thought a fact or an opinion?

  The thought 'Oh no, not again. I can't bear it. I know how it's going to end. F***ing H*ll' is both but 'I can't bear it' is just how I feel. I have to bear it. I have no choice.

P – Practise What Works – Proceed

- What is the best thing to do right now? For me? For others? For the situation?

  Do what I know I SHOULD do which is stay calm, ignore it, offer comfort and if I feel like I am losing it then walk away, if Kai is safe, until I regain my composure.

- What can I do that fits with my values?

  Do the above – stay calm and if I can't stay calm, walk away until I can. Explain to Kai that I am not leaving him but am just taking a moment so I can work out how to help him best.

- Do what will be effective and appropriate

  Easier said than done but I think giving myself permission to take a break from the situation will be helpful.

Exercise 5.1: Trying to STOPP

Try your own STOPP. Not all the questions will be helpful so don't feel like you have to answer them all but think about a difficult and ongoing situation in which it would be good for you to be able to stay calm.

S – Stop!

T – Take a Breath

O – Observe

P – Pull Back, Put in Some Perspective

P – Practise What Works – Proceed

What situation did you try STOPP in?

What was helpful?

What can you do to make it more helpful?

CHAPTER 5: SUMMARY AND KEY MESSAGES

- STOPP is a key technique from cognitive behavioural therapy that can help you manage your emotions in the moment

- STOPP stands for:

  ◊ Stop
  ◊ Take a Breath
  ◊ Observe
  ◊ Pull Back, Put in Some Perspective
  ◊ Practise What Works – Proceed

- It's easier said than done but practising will help

6: Ways of thinking

If this isn't your first self-help book, then you might be familiar with the idea of thinking styles and unhelpful ways of thinking that are often called 'errors'. If it is the first time you have come across the idea, then prepare to be amazed by the strange ways in which humans think and process information! Unhelpful ways of thinking were first properly described in the 1970s by Aaron Beck, the founding father of cognitive therapy, in his book on how to help emotional disorders. The idea is that thinking 'errors' are unhelpful patterns of thinking, and that identifying the thinking errors is the first step to helping you think differently and cope better with challenging situations. At the heart of cognitive therapy is the idea that the situation is the same, but your interpretation of the situation changes. And changing that interpretation is the key to coping because it can help to change the feelings and unhelpful behaviours (such as avoidance) that get in the way. Thinking errors are closely related to each other and also related to the STOPP technique in the previous chapter, particularly in terms of OBSERVE. They are also very relevant to the next chapter on Stress and coping. If you recognise that these thinking errors are part of your life, and you suffer with depression and anxiety, then we have some recommended reading in the Further resources section. This chapter is designed just to give you some information about common thinking errors so that you can spot them and try to find a more balanced perspective.

Common thinking errors

There are many thinking errors that have been identified, but the top five that can impact on our ability to cope are below.

1) All or nothing thinking. This is also known as 'black and white' thinking. This is a common problem when it comes to trying to cope when your child cannot.

You are not alone: Carli's all or nothing thinking

Carli was a mum of four boys and one girl. Her partner worked long hours to earn enough money to put food on the table. Carli was the primary caregiver looking after the children. The children were all quite close in age, and her eldest two struggled with dyslexia; as a result, they hated school and learning. They often fought and played truant. They hadn't been diagnosed with dyslexia until they were thirteen and fifteen and, once diagnosed, Carli felt very upset and guilty that she hadn't realised earlier and got them help. She felt that if she had, then she would have been a good parent but because she hadn't, then she was a bad parent. She felt that spotting it earlier would have meant they were successful at school, but that now they were going to fail. She became upset by her own distress and had lots of thoughts about 'if I can't cope perfectly, then I'm not coping at all'.

What can be helpful with all or nothing thinking is to try to remember the 'grey' area in between. It's strange, but just drawing a line with the 'all' thought on one end and the 'nothing' thought on the other can be helpful. For Carli, her line had 'bad parent' on one end and 'fantastic parent' on the other. In between she put 'OK' parent and she numbered the line from 0 at the 'bad parent' end to 10 at the 'fantastic parent' end, with the numbers 1–9 in between. Initially, she thought she was a bad parent but then thought about the fact that she fed her kids, clothed them, sent them to school, bought them birthday presents and read them stories. She thought about some other parents she knew who she thought were really not good parents, and some others that she felt were really doing their best and giving their children a safe home that was loving. She knew in her heart that she had created a safe and loving home for the children, and she moved her rating from being 0 'bad parent' to 7, much closer to the 'fantastic' parent end.

2) Catastrophising. When we feel as though we cannot cope, our thinking focuses on the negative and we think about the worst possible outcome of any situation. This can involve pictures in our head as well as thoughts. So, for example, in Carli's case, she was thinking about a negative future for her children rather than thinking that her children will be able to get the help and support that they need. When it comes to thoughts about coping, common catastrophising thoughts include:

- It will never get better

- I can't cope at the moment; it's only going to get worse

- If this is what it is like now, it'll be unbearable in the future

The STOPP technique can help find alternative ways of thinking and bring a different perspective, but just identifying the thinking error can be helpful in itself. Thoughts (and feelings) are not facts. Reminding yourself of the importance of 'one step at a time', 'this too shall pass', and 'nothing stays the same forever' can be helpful. It's also helpful to remind yourself that you have coped in the past, even when you didn't think you could. The fact that you have support networks that can help you and you are not alone can also give you the strength to help STOPP the thoughts and try to get a more balanced way of thinking.

3) Overgeneralisation. This is the name given to the thinking error that occurs when one instance of something is used to make broad predictions. So, for example, if you lost your temper when your child has been rude to you for the umpteenth time, you thinking, 'I'm always losing my temper, I can't cope, I'm at the end of my rope' would be overgeneralisation. Carli was overgeneralising in response to her sons' being diagnosed with dyslexia.

You are not alone: Carli's overgeneralisation

'I thought that because I had missed the dyslexia, there were other things that I must have missed that would have made me a better mum. I found it very hard to manage thinking about all the other things I might have missed. Once I started looking for 'clues' to what I had missed, I found them. I thought about how I wasn't coping with the housework, how I often gave my kids rubbish meals when I was feeling tired. I came to the conclusion that I was rubbish at everything.'

Again, spotting the thinking error is the first step to gaining perspective. It can also be helpful to ask yourself what you would say to a friend who had missed their sons' dyslexia and who was managing to raise five children with little income. You'd probably tell them how great they were, and how it was wonderful that the boys' dyslexia had been identified while still in school to enable them to get support. You might even google some facts – one in ten people have dyslexia, many are not diagnosed until adulthood and that famous, very high-achieving people like Einstein had dyslexia too.

4) Personalisation. Personalisation is particularly relevant to being a parent coping with a child who is struggling. It refers to us taking the blame and responsibility for everything that goes wrong in our life and our child's life. It links to guilt (Chapter 11) and responsibility and seriously impacts our ability to cope. Carli described her feelings of guilt over her sons in the box below.

You are not alone: Carli's personalisation

'I actually woke up in the night with a physical feeling of guilt all over me. If only I had paid more attention, if perhaps I had only had two kids (although I obviously love them all!), if only I had been less busy, then I would have spotted it. And if I had spotted it, then I could have done something about it. I know in my head that I struggled with reading and writing, and I think I have mild dyslexia, I don't blame my mum for not spotting it. I don't really even blame the school for not spotting mine as it was a long time ago. I should really have said something to someone when I was at school, but I was too ashamed. I know that in this day and age, the school should have spotted the kids' problems earlier and it isn't up to me as I'm not a teacher, but I do still feel bad.'

Thinking about all the other people responsible for the situation and improving it (including health professionals, partners, your child if old enough) can be a helpful reminder that it isn't all on your shoulders.

5) Discounting the positive. Gratitude journals are popular, and they are based on the notion that it is hard to notice the positive, but that it is something we should value. For many of us, we notice every time we lose our temper, swear, do something we regret and know we shouldn't have done, say something we swore we wouldn't, cry or go to bed just overwhelmed with it all. We feel bad and guilty. And we think 'I can't cope'. The reality is, however, that there are many, many more times when we didn't cry, swear, lose our temper, do the wrong thing or go to bed in a state. There are times when we have walked away, taken a deep breath, talked to our friends and done the 'healthy coping' covered in the next chapter.

Noticing and valuing those positives instead of mentally filtering them out, will help change your belief from 'I can't cope' to 'I am breathing; therefore, I am coping – it's just that I am human'.

Exercise 6.1: Spotting and changing your ways of thinking

Think back to a recent time when you felt like you couldn't cope.

What thoughts went through your mind at the time?

....

....

....

Looking back now, can you identify one of the five unhelpful ways of thinking (thinking errors) described (all or nothing thinking, catastrophising, overgeneralisation, personalisation and discounting the positive)? If so, write them down:

....

....

....

What changes can you make next time you are in a similar situation, e.g., would you draw a line between the two ends of the extremes for 'all or nothing thinking' to help identify the middle area?

....

....

....

If you can, make those changes and write below what happened.

....

....

....

CHAPTER 6: SUMMARY AND KEY MESSAGES

- As human beings, our thinking is not always logical

- Common thinking errors identified in cognitive therapy are:

    ◊   All or nothing thinking
    ◊   Catastrophising
    ◊   Overgeneralisation
    ◊   Personalisation
    ◊   Discounting the positive

- Identifying the unhelpful ways of thinking and using the strategies in the chapter can be helpful

7: Stress and coping

You may often marvel at how other people manage to cope so brilliantly with what seems like an unmanageable amount on their plate. And sometimes, possibly, you may be surprised at how poorly someone else, or you yourself, appears to cope with what seems to be a trivial stress. Most people will have experienced stress at some point. Richard Lazarus and colleagues have done a great deal of work in this area and stress can be considered in different ways as follows:

STRESS: when the demands on us exceed our resources, or

STRESS: a state of mental or emotional strain or tension resulting from adverse or demanding circumstances.

The other side of stress is 'coping', which can be considered as follows:

COPING: **dealing successfully with a difficult situation**

Of crucial importance to coping is how a person appraises or interprets the stressor. For example, if your child is yelling that you are the worst parent, then you could appraise it in any of the following ways.

Positive: My child is expressing their anger to me, in a safe place. So much better than doing it at school. I have a good relationship with my child that allows this to happen.

Dangerous: My child can't control her emotions, she's hysterical, she going to lose control and hurt someone outside the house and will end up in jail or worse.

Irrelevant: Is this what I signed up for as a parent?!

After that initial appraisal, there is some more thinking that goes on about the resources available to us.

Insufficient resources: I just cannot take any more of this.

Sufficient resources: 'Sticks and stones' – let her yell, it makes no odds to me.

The level of stress depends on the relationship between the stress and resources, and there are two main coping methods.

Problem-focused: Changing the situation itself. This is where the problem-solving that we described in Chapter 3 can help.

Emotion-focused: Changing the reaction to the situation; this is what this book is designed to help with, using strategies such as STOPP and identifying thinking errors.

You may have heard of the 'stress bucket' which is illustrated overleaf and shows the relationship between stress and coping.

Knowing your own limits: Stress and coping

We are human. We all have our own limitations and, ultimately, limited influence over our children's lives. The bucket analogy can be a helpful way to think about stress. The diagram below is taken from The Charity for Civil Servants (https://foryoubyyou.org.uk/stress-bucket).

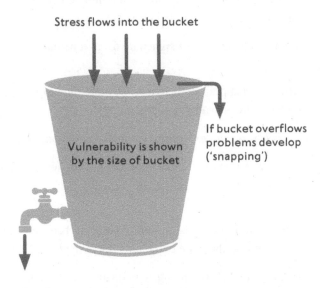

Stress flows into the bucket

Vulnerability is shown by the size of bucket

If bucket overflows problems develop ('snapping')

Good coping: tap working – lets the stress out
Bad coping: tap not working – water fills the bucket

Untangling your coping and theirs

In addition to being parents, we are also people. It may be that you consider your child's sadness and inability to cope to be the main cause of your own, but it is also possible that you have your own independent issues that are making you sad and making it hard to cope. You may be sad for many reasons – your relationships, your health, your genetics, your experiences, your way of looking at the world, your finances and so on . . . Understanding your own emotions and the impact that they have on you and your child is going to be beneficial to everyone. You may decide that you want some therapy for yourself to better help you understand your sadness and help you cope, or you may read books or talk to others. Understanding your own experiences and taking the time to do so will benefit your child (see Further resources).

Coping is quite complicated. Some strategies may help in the short-term e.g., avoiding a difficult situation, but prove unhelpful in the longer term.

Finally, it is important to remember the basics. Making sure you are eating properly, sleeping and getting exercise are all fundamental aspects of healthy coping.

You are not alone: Yoma's story

'I know it is obvious, but I find I cope so much better after a good night's sleep. I get terrible headaches if I don't sleep properly, and the same with eating. That's probably the single most important factor that affects how I cope (or don't) with the challenges that I face every day with Tiba's disability. I need physical and emotional strength to put Tiba in the wheelchair, to sort out the respite care and so on. I am so much more irritable and stressed if I don't sleep. I don't always manage it – Tiba sleeps very little and that impacts hugely – but I do try to prioritise it.'

Some examples of longer term helpful and unhelpful coping are given below.

Helpful coping	Unhelpful coping
Exercise	Drugs or alcohol
Sharing your problems with a friend	Overeating or under eating
Acceptance	Avoidance or procrastination
Time management	Denial
Getting support from a professional	Losing your temper
Noticing small pleasures	Becoming violent
Problem-solving	Making threats that you won't carry out
Relaxation strategies, e.g., listening to music	Sleeping too little
Using parenting strategies when needed	Quitting
Getting the information you need to help think rationally	Focusing on the negative
Doing something you enjoy, e.g., watching cute cat videos on the internet, doing some art, reading a magazine	Putting yourself down all the time
Reaching out to your community, e.g., religious community	Blaming yourself
Challenging your thinking	Cutting yourself
Yoga and meditation	

7: Stress and coping

It is helpful to think about a current specific problem you are trying to cope with. You may want to choose something you identified from the chapter on problem-solving. That chapter goes well with this one as the coping strategies can be used to help identify some alternative solutions and ways of coping. Completing the exercise below may help you think about how some of the helpful strategies above can be applied to help you cope.

Exercise 7.1: Identifying your helpful and unhelpful coping strategies	
What problem are you trying to cope with at the moment?	
What strategies have you tried that are unhelpful?	What has happened?

What strategies could you try that may be helpful?	What needs to happen to help you try them?

CHAPTER 7: SUMMARY AND KEY MESSAGES

- When the demands on us exceed our ability to manage them, we feel stressed

- Some ways of coping are more helpful than others

- Use the strategies here with those in other sections such as problem-solving to help identify the ways of coping that are most helpful for you

8: How vs. why

Some interesting work by a clinical psychologist and researcher specialising in depression, Professor Ed Watkins, has made an important distinction between 'how' questions and 'why' questions. His work has focused on repetitive thinking such as worry and rumination when the same thoughts go round and round in our heads. Such thinking is associated with questions such as, 'What does this say about me?', 'Why can't I handle things better?', 'Why did this happen to me?' These types of questions are associated with low mood and anxiety, as well as health problems. Everyone has this type of thinking and it can sometimes be helpful. The key is to distinguish between when this thinking is helpful for making a useful plan, and when it is unhelpful because it is an unanswerable question. Just telling yourself to stop worrying won't work, but what can work is focusing on a 'how' question rather than a 'why' question. Take the example below.

You are not alone: Shareen's story

Shareen had three children, all with a range of special needs. She was hugely busy and overwhelmed with the demands on her from morning until night. In between her various chores, she would ask herself why she had three children who all had special needs, why her partner was unable to support her other than 'just' going to work, and why she was being punished. She felt utterly miserable most of the time. After getting some professional help, Shareen tried to change the questions into 'how'. She practised asking the questions 'How can I get my husband to help?', 'How can I get the support I need from other people?', and 'How can I get just a little bit of pleasure back in my life?'

Caring what other people think

A lot of stress is caused by caring too much what other people think. When you have a child who is unhappy, it can be hard to keep that within close family and friends. And you may be a very private person who doesn't want the school to know what is going on, or you may feel judged at the school gate if your child is missing a lot of school. You may imagine the whispers about what a terrible parent you must be if you can't even get your child to school. Or whispers about how you could possibly let your child become overweight, or so underweight, or dye their hair, or have a tattoo, or drink so much, or not drink enough . . . When your child is rude to you in front of other people, it's embarrassing and can play on your mind long after the event has passed. It is challenging but caring less what other people think can really make a difference because, in reality, many of the things affecting your child are beyond your control.

There are books on this topic entitled *How to Give Zero F*cks* (by Stephen Wildish) and *The Subtle Art of Not Giving a F*ck* (by Mark Manson) but if we had to give one brief, top tip on how to manage this, then it would be to just ask yourself 'What would I be thinking or saying if it were a friend in that position?' If your friend had a child who was refusing to go to school, what would you be thinking? Probably, 'Poor her, she must really be having a hideous time'. If it were your friend whose child was staying out and drinking, you would probably be thinking, 'She must be worried sick, what a stressful situation'. You cannot mind-read what other people are thinking but the bottom line is that your friends and the good people in the world will be feeling for you, not judging you. And the key is to try to find the compassion for yourself in the same way as you would for a friend (see Chapter 10). Is it the case that they are disapproving of you or are you disapproving of yourself and imagine they feel the same way? As for the rest of them, their views don't matter and are a distraction from your task of supporting your child through their unhappiness and making sure you have the inner strength to take care of yourself too.

Exercise 8.1: Changing 'why' questions to 'how' questions

Think back to a recent time when you found yourself stuck going over and over a specific event.

Did you ask yourself 'why questions'? If so, how did that make you feel?

....

....

What do you think would have happened if you had asked yourself 'how' questions?

....

....

Can you think of a situation coming up that might lead to rumination? If so, try to use 'how' questions instead of 'why' questions when going over it in your mind. If you manage to do that, write down the impact on how you felt.

....

....

CHAPTER 8: SUMMARY AND KEY MESSAGES

- Asking 'why' questions can be unhelpful and can mean you keep going over the same issues in your head

- Replacing 'why' questions with 'how' questions may be a simple but helpful strategy

9: Multitasking and time management

Multitasking is the default mode of every parent, we suspect. And it seems to us that multitasking is the only way that we can get through the list of tasks that need to be completed when your child is sad and needs so much of your time to comfort them. But the science tells us that multitasking is actually unhelpful. Take looking at your phone when doing homework. The research says that it makes studying worse and also impacts on sleep. Some tasks – such as talking on the phone in front of the TV – may not place too much demand on us, but making dinner at the same time as helping the kids, tidying up, texting a friend and looking for the lost car keys is just too much. If you think about the last time you forgot something, it was probably because of multitasking. Multitasking can make us feel as though we aren't doing anything properly and gives a sense that things are just out of control.

So, what is a better way to try to get all the stuff done that really needs doing?

Increasing your efficiency

If we could give you more hours in the day, we would. But we can't. So, within the limited amount of time available, how can we be more efficient? The 'Eisenhower' is a time management matrix in which you divide tasks into important tasks, not important tasks, urgent tasks and not urgent tasks. An example is below.

Eisenhower matrix example

	Urgent	Not urgent
Important	Completing a project by the deadline	Changing the oil in your car
Not Important	Getting one of the free doughnuts in the break room	Commenting on pictures of funny cats

You are not alone: Felipe's story

Take Felipe. Felipe was working from home during the COVID-19 pandemic, at the same time as his daughter Zoey, aged sixteen, was doing online schooling in preparation for her exams. Felipe wanted to help her and needed to work, but as a single dad he also had to make sure that there was food in the house (online shopping slots were impossible to book) and deliver food to his elderly mother who was shielding. Everything seemed important and everything seemed urgent. It was overwhelming. Felipe used the matrix to help organise his priorities.

	Urgent	Not urgent
Important	I need to do my work, or I will get fired. No choice here. Zoey needs to get her work done.	Getting food for the family; I do have some pasta in the house. They won't starve if they don't have their first choice of what to eat. I can go shopping on Saturday and then take the food to Mum's straight after and bring Zoey with me. Going to Mike's drinks.
Not Important		Sorting out the cupboards.

Looking at the matrix helped Felipe prioritise and organise his time. It also helped him realise that although everything was important, there were different amounts of urgency so he could think and plan ahead. He decided only to go to Mike's drinks for a short time and to arrange a catch-up call with Mike after Zoey's exams because he recognised that in the longer-term, keeping up his social support was very important (just not as urgent). It is important to recognise that time to look after yourself, time spent planning, is actually an investment of time and will help you complete your other tasks better. Being exhausted, angry, frustrated and emotional will slow you down and make you worse at other tasks, so please make sure that looking after yourself is put in the 'Important' section of the grid!

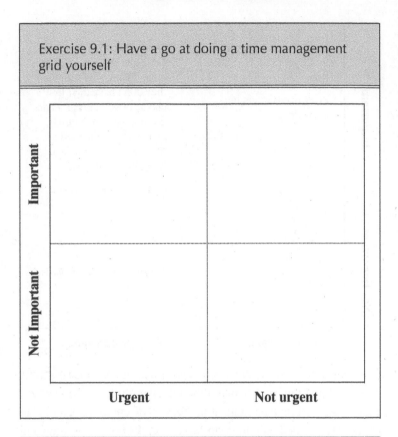

Exercise 9.1: Have a go at doing a time management grid yourself

	Urgent	Not urgent
Important		
Not Important		

CHAPTER 9: SUMMARY AND KEY MESSAGES

- We are busy so end up multitasking

- Multitasking may be unhelpful and inefficient

- A time management matrix can help make the most of the time we have

- Separating important and urgent tasks is key

10: Empathy and compassion

We tend to be very self-critical and harsh on ourselves, although the science shows that being kind to ourselves is important and works. But how? We are probably much harder on ourselves than we are on other people. We are full of 'shoulds'. We have a lot of 'musts'. One of the most influential psychologists and founders of a type of therapy called 'Rational Emotive Behavior Therapy', Albert Ellis, called this 'musterabation'. I must do this, I must do that, I must do the other. And our lives are full of shoulds and musts. When you have a child who is unhappy, there are even more shoulds and musts, and it is relentless.

You are not alone: Chloe's story

Chloe woke up every morning with a headache and a massive 'to do' list. She got up an hour before everyone else, just to get everything ready as she had the belief that she should have everything organised before everyone else got up. She did her hair and make-up every day, got dressed in freshly ironed clothes, and cleaned the house. She did all of this while managing two part-time jobs and two children. She spent hours with the children, hours with housework, just trying to make things as good as they could possibly be. When something didn't go according to plan, e.g., the dishes weren't done, the children were upset or she had forgotten something or had made a mistake at work, Chloe felt terrible. She was hugely self-critical and felt she deserved the names she called herself ('F**k Up' was her favourite nickname for herself). It made her miserable, but she also felt that criticising herself in this way gave her motivation to try to do better next time.

The science doesn't support Chloe's idea that self-criticism helps motivate people to do better. In fact, it is the opposite. It makes people feel miserable and unmotivated.

If you are self-critical, then you may want to look at the self-compassion website by Kristin Neff (https://self-compassion.org/) and some other reading (see Further resources). The website has a questionnaire for you to assess your levels of self-compassion and exercises to help. Two of our favourite exercises to help with self-kindness are described in Exercise 10.1.

Exercise 10.1: Exercises to help with self-compassion

1. Ask what you would say to a friend who is in the same situation. Would you be kinder to them? Why do you have double standards? Can you adjust yours so that they are fair, and the same rules apply to you as they do to others?
2. Write a letter to yourself to help express compassion. Some guidance is below.

    a. Think about something about yourself that you dislike or that makes you criticise yourself – it may be a feeling that you should cope better than you do, it could be you feel inadequate, or jealous or any other area.

b. Write down what it is about yourself that leads you to self-criticism and describe your feelings. For example, if you feel jealousy of other people, perhaps that makes you feel guilty. Your child's struggles may lead you to feel embarrassment.

c. Write a letter to yourself expressing compassion, under-standing and acceptance for the part of yourself that you are criticising. The following suggestions for writing the letter may be helpful.

    i. Imagine that there is someone who loves and accepts you completely and unconditionally for you as a person. What would they say about this part of yourself?

    ii. Think broadly about how many other people may also be experiencing these negative emotions and characteristics but aren't telling other people; remind yourself that flaws are part of human nature.

    iii. Try to think about your experiences growing up, or your genetics, and how they may have contributed to this negative part of yourself and how that is not your fault.

    iv. With kindness and compassion, ask yourself if there are things that you can do to help manage this negative aspect of yourself (hopefully some of the techniques in the book will be useful here). Think about how constructive changes may help you cope better and feel better about the situation you find yourself in and the emotions you experience.

    v. After writing the letter, leave it for a while and then come back to it with a sense of kindness and com-passion as you re-read and perhaps add to it.

You are not alone:
Lin's letter to herself to express compassion

Not being a good enough parent to my son:

This is something I struggle with most days. A sense that I am a better parent to my daughter than to my son. That I give her more rope, am more emotionally available for her, notice her achievements and name them far more readily than those of my son.

This makes me feel dreadfully guilty. That I have also, over time, contributed to his problems by not being there enough for him. That if I was able to show my love for him more, and rejoice in him more, he would be less unhappy, and a more virtuous cycle would be taking place. I also worry that I have damaged him 'for life'. That my negative behaviours in this regard, when he was younger, are things that have formed him and that it's too late to make amends. I fear I have been blindsided and it has come out as favouring one child above the other. Which feels unforgiveable. I feel really sad and anxious and guilty about this, and dwelling on it makes me miserable. I want to compensate but whenever I try and connect or even apologise I feel a fraud.

My best friend would say this to me:

You do love your son; you always have done. I remember you with him shortly after he was born; you were elated and yet so anxious, you knew your world would never be the same again. It had been a very difficult birth and feeding issues were enormous. You tried so hard to do things right, to breast-feed when it was extremely difficult. He took six weeks to start putting on weight, you were beside yourself during this time; a battle you hadn't seen coming straight after the trauma of childbirth. Your first child too.

10: Empathy and compassion

You asked for help in all the right places, you put that baby at the front and centre of your life and have continued to do so ever since. It hasn't always been easy. You have had many hiccups along the way, as all lives do, and he has found life additionally hard in places. I have heard you blame yourself for having an epidural when he was born, for the few minutes that he got 'stuck' and wondering if you had managed without pain relief if he would have been born without the 'processing' issues that have made school and friendships so difficult for him at times.

All births are a lottery, you did your best to bring him into the world. And have been there for him ever since. You and your family have done so much to try and help him with every aspect of his development, and he is a lovely young man. Hardworking, kind and thoughtful. He hasn't a mean bone in his body. You do also communicate well as a family, from what I see. He knows he is loved and that you are available for him. He can (and does) call you when he needs to. He is ambitious and has pushed himself far further than anyone at school ever thought he would. They thought he wouldn't get into higher education and he has proved everyone wrong. Along the way, you have given him the confidence and environment and ambition to keep working and believe in himself. Without putting on any undue pressure, at any point. He has found this hard-working seam for himself, and it's wonderful to see.

You have provided opportunities for him that he has taken up. And you are still very much there for her him when he falls. The guilt you feel is also a sign of the love you feel. By acknowledging that he hasn't always been the favourite (and there is a taboo subject if there ever was one), you are showing self-awareness that means you are always aware of the balancing act, and not acting out on your favouritism thoughts, even if they are there. You are always adjusting and thinking about this. That is not the act of a selfish and disregarding parent, capable of wreaking careless damage.

You have also spoken to him openly about this as he has got older; he knows how much you both love him, and always have done. Also, I think it is worth mentioning that his father possibly balances the scales here. He has always been great with both kids but would probably say he 'gets' him better. So, there is a parenting balance that can be noted and is probably there in most families. Also, it shifts through different ages and stages.

He has seen you both struggling as parents from time to time. But he has also heard you apologising and been part of very meaningful conversations about getting things back on track and making the whole family work as well as possible, as a unit. Think of the many benefits of 'rupture and repair' – the idea that it's healthy for children to see things go wrong and be fixed again, like seeing parents disagree and make up – that mean it's in many ways better than never seeing any discord.

CHAPTER 10: SUMMARY AND KEY MESSAGES

- 'Shoulds' and 'musts' can make us highly self-critical

- Self-criticism is unhelpful

- Being kind to ourselves doesn't always come naturally but writing a self-compassion letter and treating ourselves as we would treat our friends can be helpful

11: Guilt

Anxiety and depression get a lot of attention in the newspapers and online, and although the previous chapters in this section apply for lots of emotions, they have mainly come from work on feelings such as low mood and worries. Our emotions are more complicated than that, and many of us just feel 'upset'. Such feelings of 'upset' can be made up of several different feelings and thoughts all mixed up together in a giant mess. This chapter discusses some of the everyday feelings that it is helpful to think about and try to change, despite very difficult circumstances. The next few chapters focus on those complicated feelings such as guilt, shame and embarrassment, responsibility and control, jealousy and anger. People's stories are described to help show that if you have these types of feelings, you are not alone. The stories, together with the tried and tested strategies, are designed to bring hope and help.

Guilt

You are not alone: Annika's story

'I feel that the expression "damned if I do, damned if I don't" sums up my life. Whatever I do, it will be the wrong thing. If I devote my time to Kyra, then I feel guilty about neglecting my other children. If I pay attention to the other kids, then I feel guilty about Kyra. I know I am supposed

> *to look after myself but, honestly, I feel so guilty if I do that it just isn't worth it. I feel guilty I am not doing anything properly. I even feel guilty for feeling guilty.'*

Annika's strong sense of guilt is common to most parents, but parenting a child who has particular emotional, developmental, behavioural or other needs is especially challenging. On the 'to do' list of life, looking after yourself can be pretty close to the bottom. The previous chapters all show that it is fundamentally important to take the time for small pleasures, to try to manage your own emotions, to invest time to think differently and so on. But guilt can stop us from doing that. It can just feel wrong to put your needs above your child's in the short term, even if in the longer term you know rationally that it is in your child's best interests.

We won't sit here and argue again that it is in your child's best interests to look after yourself, but instead we suggest it is worth taking some time to look at why it is so difficult to do so. And guilt, shame, embarrassment, responsibility, jealousy, anger and control all come into play. Tackling these will help you to try to stay afloat yourself so you can be there to support your child through his/her difficulties.

What is guilt? Guilt is considered as the feeling of worry or unhappiness that you have because you have done something wrong, such as causing harm to another person. It happens in response to breaking moral standards. It is when there is a 'should' rule in your life that you break. Take the examples below.

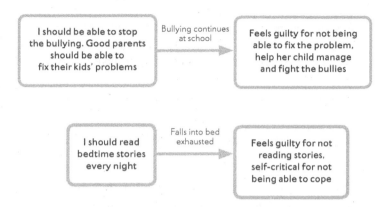

So, guilt is meant to work in the past. But it can actually work together with worrying to make people feel guilty about situations that haven't even happened yet. Such 'anticipatory' guilt is surprisingly common as shown below.

You are not alone: Sasha's story

Sasha had had enough. While she loved her son Tolu (aged fourteen), he was hard work. He was demanding, messy and mostly ungrateful. He was also impulsive and was often in trouble in school. At home, he could be very withdrawn, and Sasha suspected he was depressed. About a year ago, she had taken Tolu to the GP who said that he would make a referral to child mental health services, but Tolu refused, and Sasha didn't have the energy to fight him and also thought it was pointless to have an appointment that he wouldn't go to. In private, alone at night, Sasha was overwhelmed with feeling guilty that she didn't have enough strength to have fought for Tolu to go to the child mental health services, and that his problems had continued for so long. She worried about his future – she feared he wouldn't get any qualifications, wouldn't get a job and it would be all her fault for being such a weak mother. She already felt guilty about what she was worried would be his 'wasted' life, even though he wasn't even sitting any exams for another two years.

What can be done to help?

Under normal circumstances, when someone feels guilty for something they have done, there are actions that can be taken to try to 'repair' the harm. You can apologise, do something to make the situation better, buy flowers, etc. But when it comes to feeling guilty for not being a 'good enough' parent, what are the options?

We would suggest one helpful strategy is to look at your rules, 'shoulds' and 'musts'. Are they reasonable? Is it humanly possible to be a good parent all the time, to fix your child's problems? Are you trying your best under incredibly difficult circumstances? You can work out if your rules, 'shoulds' and 'musts', are reasonable by talking to other parents whose children are in the same situation as yours. If you have a child with a disability, what is reasonable to expect from yourself? Parenting is a marathon, not a sprint. Dealing with a long-term problem requires different rules and expectations. Even better than having rules, 'shoulds' and 'should-nots', is to think about having *guidelines*. The difference between a rule and a guideline is that rules break and guidelines bend. After breaking a rule, you feel guilty. You can't break a guideline. Take the following examples below.

Rule	Guideline
I should always make a healthy dinner for the kids	I can try to make healthy dinners for the kids but sometimes an unhealthy take out is OK
I must always be there for the kids physically and emotionally	I prefer to be there for the children when I can but sometimes it just isn't possible
The children's needs should always come before mine	I prefer to put children's needs before mine but it's OK if sometimes that can't happen
I should make sacrifices for the kids	Sometimes I will need to make sacrifices for the children, but it is a choice
The children's happiness comes before mine	It's OK to sometimes put my happiness first

Exercise 11.1: Changing Rules into Guidelines

List your rules, 'shoulds' and 'musts'.

Now think of the alternative guideline for each rule.

Rule	Guideline

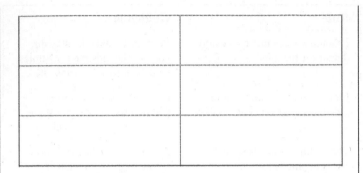

Once you have done this, the next step is to put those guidelines into practice. It is not enough just to think of the guideline but try to spend a day really living as though you believed that guideline. So instead of your rules and musts, you had a gentler guideline. What was the impact? Were you a worse parent? Or were you a happier person and a better parent?

CHAPTER 11: SUMMARY AND KEY MESSAGES

- Guilt is a common reaction that stems from breaking a moral standard and feeling as though you have done something wrong

- Transforming rigid rules into flexible guidelines can help you live your life with less guilt, but it takes practice

12: Shame and embarrassment

Just as Sasha (previous chapter) was anticipating guilt, it is the thought of embarrassment that affects much of what we do. Nobody likes their child to be the one screaming at the check-out. It is embarrassing, shaming or even humiliating, when your child shows off to their friends by being rude or insulting to you. It gives rise to lots of complicated emotions all together, but shame and embarrassment are the big ones.

You are not alone: Merina's story

Merina's daughter, Su, was nine years old and had traits of autism spectrum disorder. She was high functioning and in mainstream school, but she struggled with making friends, with changes in routine, and she particularly disliked crowds and loud noises. Cafés and coffee shops were particularly difficult for Su, so Merina avoided going whenever possible. When they were unavoidable, like on a long journey, or when they were waiting for a hospital appointment, Merina would choose the quietest one possible and sit near the door in case she had to leave. More often than not, Su would become upset and scream, and Merina always left immediately, often before she had finished (or sometimes started) her coffee. She couldn't stand the embarrassment of people looking at

---

> her and Su. Most times after this happened, she would lie awake at night and she could feel her cheeks flushing just at the memory of people looking at her.

Embarrassment and shame go together. Embarrassment is feeling very self-conscious and shame is described in the dictionary as 'a painful emotion caused by the belief that one is, or is perceived by others to be, inferior or unworthy of affection or respect because of one's actions, thoughts, circumstances or experience'. It may be irrational, but many people feel ashamed that their child is sad or struggling. It is as though it is a reflection on them as parents. And when you have more than one child with difficulties, it feels as though that is proof that you have done something wrong as a parent (leading right back to guilt). We know people gossip, and we fear being judged. So, for Merina, even though she knew that people didn't know that Su had special needs, she still felt embarrassed and ashamed. As a result, she went out less which, in turn, affected her friendships and reduced the social support that she needed.

What can be done to help?

There is surprisingly little written on practical techniques to help with shame and embarrassment in parenting situations, but four broad areas may be useful.

1) Acceptance. Section 5 discusses the importance of acceptance and such strategies are likely to be useful when addressing shame and embarrassment.

2) Self-compassion. This was addressed in Chapter 10. As a reminder, there are good books written about being kind and compassionate to yourself, and the work of Paul Gilbert (https://www.compassionatemind.co.uk/) on the compassionate mind and Kristin Neff (https://self-compassion.org/) on self-compassion are particularly useful (see also Further resources). There are more top tips at https://positivepsychology.com/how-to-practice-self-compassion/. The aim of all of this work is to be less self-critical and to be kinder to yourself; to show yourself empathy and silence your self-critic.

3) Refocusing attention. There is a lot of research on people with social anxiety, who suffer a great deal with feelings of embarrassment and shame. Social anxiety can make a person focus a great deal of attention inwards on themself in stressful social situations. This self-focused attention increases access to negative thoughts and feelings, and it prevents the person from observing external information that might be different from their beliefs. So, for example, it may be that if Merina was able to look around the coffee shop, she would see that people were not looking at her but chatting to each other. Or if they were looking, it may be that they were looking with an expression of concern rather than judgement. The research suggests that people with social anxiety have an image in their heads of what they must look like to other people (frazzled, red-faced, incompetent) which is different from the reality. Being able to try incredibly hard to take a deep breath and calm down physically helps with that image, and focusing attention outwardly can also be helpful.

As always, such refocusing of attention is easier said than done.

Exercise 12.1: Refocusing attention

Next time you are in a situation that could be potentially embarrassing and shameful, focus your attention entirely on yourself. Focus on how flustered you feel, and how embarrassed. Don't look around you. Make a note of how you think you came across, and your levels of shame and embarrassment.

The time after that when you are in a situation that is potentially embarrassing and shameful, focus your attention outwardly. Focus on other people, or the wallpaper or *anything* except yourself. Look around you. Make a note of how you think you came across, and your levels of shame and embarrassment.

If you feel that it is helpful to refocus your attention outwards rather than inwards, then this is a quick strategy that can help reduce shame and embarrassment.

---

4) Caring less what others think. This is the key. But it's very hard to do. Sometimes it comes with experience and age. Sometimes it never comes at all. The strategies we have discussed in the book so far and the chapter on acceptance can all be helpful. Another technique is to consider the pros and cons of caring what others think. An example is below.

You are not alone: Charla's story

Charla was mum to a three-year-old toddler, Dean. Dean was 'lively', and his mum suspected he had attention deficit hyperactivity disorder (ADHD). He was always saying 'no' to everything.

Even the smallest request was met with 'no'. 'Get in the car please now, Dean'. 'No', he would respond. 'Brush your teeth please now, Dean'. 'No', he would respond. Charla and Dean constantly argued. Charla had tried lots of parenting strategies and sometimes they worked for a while, and sometimes they didn't. They were hard to do. Charla was thoroughly miserable, as she was someone that really cared what other people thought of her. She was ashamed that she couldn't make her three-year-old son do even the basics and often cried herself to sleep at night thinking what a useless parent she was. She felt so bad about herself, she decided she shouldn't have any more children.

In addition to the other strategies in the book, Charla reviewed the pros and cons of caring what other people thought. Her list is below.

Pros	Cons
If I care what others think, then I will be a better member of society	It makes me miserable
	It stops me going out
	I am always embarrassed
	I feel judged all the time
	I won't have another baby in case (s)he has the same problems as Dean

Charla could see the disadvantages far outweighed the advantages. She tried to think differently about the situation. She decided her priority was Dean and that it was important for Dean to go out to the different places and to try to learn how to behave. Avoiding them wasn't fair on him. Not having a sibling wasn't fair on him. So, Charla tried really hard when she was in difficult situations to have something she could say to herself. She came up with the following self-statement:

'Dean is what matters, not other people who don't know us.'

Exercise 12.2: Changing how much you care about what others think

Write a list of pros and cons about your caring what other people think. At the end, come up with your own 'self-statement' that you can use in difficult situations.

Pros	Cons

Self-statement:

CHAPTER 12: SUMMARY AND KEY MESSAGES

- Shame and embarrassment often go together and are not often spoken about openly

- Four strategies can be helpful:

  ◊ Acceptance

  ◊ Self-compassion

  ◊ Refocusing attention

  ◊ Caring less what others think

13: Responsibility

Klari's story

'I was always stressed, couldn't sleep and felt utterly exhausted. I was constantly irritable, grumpy, busy, bitter and resentful. I was often ill with migraine headaches. One day, I just decided I couldn't carry on like this. I was a person too and I just didn't have a life worth living. I loved my kids and family but enough was enough. So, I decided to do things differently. When my partner told me that he hadn't found a job despite looking all day and was going to have a few beers with friends, I just said 'It's OK' rather than making suggestions of where else he could look. When my son told me he wasn't doing well at college, instead of trying to help him or get him a tutor, I just said 'It's OK, you have time to improve your marks, and you can change the subjects you are studying if you would like.' When my daughter said that she had lost her school laptop, instead of screaming, yelling and turning the house upside down, I suggested calmly that she retraced her steps, looked for it, and asked the school if she could borrow one in the meantime.

'My kids were taken aback by my calmness and the way I was dealing with the situations – not like me at all. So, I tried to explain that I had – rather belatedly – realised that everyone was responsible for their own life and situation. I can support them, but ultimately it wasn't doing *anyone any favours to take on the responsibility of each of their lives. Me taking on responsibility didn't solve their problems, but it caused me problems and, in the long run, deprived them of the ability to learn how to deal with the challenges of daily life. I realised that I can 'lead a horse to water but I can't make it drink'. I realised that I can only be responsible for myself, and my own actions, not other people's reactions. All of the self-help courses I had been on, all the reading, all the meditation, you name it, all finally led me to realise that I am not responsible for the actions of others. I cannot be as I have no control over other people. I can give my opinion and advice, but if someone doesn't take it – there isn't much I can do. Even if that person is a child and they are meant to listen to me.*

'Over time, the kids began to take more responsibility for their own actions, and I felt lighter. Some days worked better than others, but the message was clear. I'm not responsible – you are.'

Responsibility will vary with each family's circumstance but responsibility is closely related to control. Logically, you cannot be responsible for situations or people where you don't have control. Sadly, we don't have as much control as we would like in many situations. So, we cannot be held responsible. Even when responsible, we often think we have more responsibility than we do.

What can be done to help?

Some of the people reading this book will have been unable to get their children to attend school despite years of trying, tears and distress. Words can't describe the daily agony of the screaming, the involvement of school, the embarrassment and shame. It can feel as though it is 100 per cent your responsibility to get your child to school. But thinking it through in terms of who is responsible for a particular action and doing a pie-chart can be helpful.

Let's imagine an example where your child is twelve years old and refusing school. Who is responsible for getting them to attend? You? OK. Maybe you have some responsibility but let's leave you to one side for now. Who else?

1. Your child has some responsibility. How much? Maybe 10 per cent because they do understand the importance of learning.

2. Your partner has some responsibility. How much? Maybe 10 per cent as well because they have got to go to work and can't lose their job.

3. The school? How much? Well, at least 30 per cent because part of what makes it hard in this example is crowding at the school gates and schoolwork that is proving too hard. The school haven't been responsive or particularly helpful; they have seemingly not been listening to you.

4. Health professional services such as Child Mental Health Services. How much? At least 30 per cent too because you have raised this with them repeatedly; they could send someone round to help but won't because of their policies and although they are kind and try their best, they are overstretched and starved of resources.

5. What's left? Your responsibility. The amount of responsibility left is 20 per cent. Together your child, your partner, the school and services also have responsibility that adds up to 80 per cent. So, although it feels as though it is all up to you, others share the responsibility. Drawing it as a pie chart can be helpful.

13: Responsibility

Responsibility

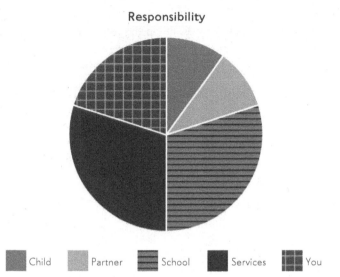

Child   Partner   School   Services   You

Exercise 13.1: Using a pie chart to change your responsibility estimates

Think of a situation where you feel responsible. Work out all the other people that may be responsible too. Divide up the pie chart. Are your feelings of responsibility reduced?

Situation:

....

....

....

....

Use the circle below to divide up the responsibility into a pie chart:

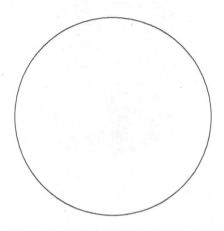

CHAPTER 13: SUMMARY AND KEY MESSAGES

- Although it may feel like managing the situation is all your responsibility, it is helpful to know your limits

- You can only influence your own behaviour and reactions, not those of others

- Drawing a pie chart to identify and divide up responsibility may be helpful

14: Jealousy and anger

Anger

Jealousy, envy, anger and rage can be overpowering emotions. They are often seen as shameful. We may vaguely identify them as on the list of the seven deadly sins. Our instinct is often to hide them, because they can feel uncontrollable and because they involve other people. They can frighten us because they are emotions that can sometimes lead to hurting other people – physically or verbally or emotionally – and that could be punishable by law. Anger-management courses exist for exactly this reason. How we or other people behave when we feel angry can be terrifying to witness and to experience. Services get involved and quickly. So, there is a great taboo surrounding anger, especially women who show anger. In many ways it is portrayed as an 'unfeminine' emotion and a woman showing anger is considered more shocking than an angry man because she is departing from the stereotypes society instils in us. The point should also be made that such anger is often directed at services – inability to access the right help at the right time and place for your child can elicit incredibly powerful and strong feelings of rage, and an intense desire to fight for what could potentially be helpful. Such anger can be based on serious genuine unfairness and collectively could be very reasonably be used for action towards change. In this way, anger can be seen as a normal and healthy emotion that comes from the sense of injustice.

Many complications arise from trying to run away from it and feel something else – anything else. This running away and avoidance is how anger hurts the person feeling it – as much, or even more than anyone else who's affected. To acknowledge the feelings of anger and engage with them is the first, essential step towards taking away anger's power over you. Seeing anger as it arises, and even directing it positively, can result in a sense of release. It needs to be experienced and processed and then dealt with.

Ray Novaco has done a lot of work on anger and it may be helpful to ask yourself the following questions based on his 'Dimensions of Anger Reactions' scale.

---

1. Do you often find yourself getting angry at people or situations in general?

2. When you get angry, do you find yourself getting really enraged and mad?

3. Do you stay angry for a long time once your anger has been triggered?

4. When you get angry, do you want to hit the person?

5. Does your anger interfere with your ability to function at work, socially or at home?

If the answers to the above questions are mostly 'yes', then it is worth spending some time on helping to manage your anger.

Top tips for anger management

1) Recognise the triggers. It's strange how the same situation can trigger anger at some times but not others. It may depend on a lot of personal factors – how tired you are, what is happening with other worries, whether you are hungry, if you have exercised. Making a note of when you are at risk is likely to be helpful.

If your child is demanding the same thing repeatedly when you have already said 'no', and this is what triggers your anger, then think about how to address that. For example, tell them you will give them an answer and if it is 'no', and they then repeat the request, they will be told 'I told you "no" and explained why earlier. I am not repeating myself'. And you will repeat that same phrase each time you are asked. It will help manage the situation but also give you a sense of control and a strategy, so you don't go down the rabbit hole of arguments and making the anger worse. You may want to monitor all the times you have become angry in the last week and make a note of the triggers to help you recognise them.

2) Identify your early warning signs. Anger, like anxiety and stress, causes a response in our bodies. Your heart may race, you may get a sense of rage just welling up from inside you. These will be early warning signs that you may be about to explode. You will have mental signs too – so make a note of them to catch them early, for example, thoughts about the unfairness of a situation, or your mind racing.

3) Use some of the strategies in the book. Using STOPP, identifying thinking styles and addressing responsibility can all be helpful for managing anger. Engaging in the small pleasures and learning acceptance is helpful too. Some people find taking slow, deep breaths helpful. More strategies can be found in the Further resources section. Ultimately, finding a way to walk away from the situation is going to be key to not making it worse.

Exercise can be helpful for some people – in reducing the likelihood of feeling overwhelming anxiety in general, and also sometimes when you can feel anger start to build. Walking, swimming, dancing . . . whatever works for you to help diffuse some of the intensity anger can involve.

You are not alone: Gabi's story

'My daughter Livi has always been 'difficult'. People say that we have spoiled her, and we probably have, but really we were only trying to manage and not be completely embarrassed all the time, so we did give in a lot. My other kids aren't like that though. Anyway, Livi came home one day in a bad mood. Normally I can ignore it, but this time she had brought her girlfriend with her, and she was being really rude to me in front of her girlfriend. She called me a 'motherf***' and a 'c**t'. I couldn't ignore it and let myself be treated like that in front of her girlfriend and my other kids. I tried to stay calm, but I could feel my hackles rising. I didn't completely lose it at first but then I just thought of all the things I have done for Livi – every minute of every day – and I just got so angry about how unfair it was that I was being humiliated in this way. And then I totally lost my cool and yelled all kinds of things that I shouldn't. We both later calmed down and talked it through (I say "later" but it took a couple of days). We agreed that if she was going to be rude to me in front of others, then I would just walk away and ignore it, and her, until she calmed

down and apologised. I wouldn't add fuel to the fire by retaliating. Instead, I would watch some comedy videos on YouTube. It goes back to the boundaries – for me Livi had crossed the line and we agreed that if I had done that to her, then she'd have been angry too.'

Jealousy and envy

Many of us feel intense jealousy and envy of other people who appear to have an easier life than us. Their children appear wildly success-ful at school, incredibly popular, and always happy and laughing. Their partners are supportive, and they can be found jogging along together splashing in the puddles. Although we can rationally tell ourselves that they must have problems like everyone else, it doesn't appear that way in the moment. We feel jealous. We want that life. We want that for our children. And it isn't likely to happen.

You are not alone: Tila's story

'The visibility of parenting in lockdown killed me. Every day, my neighbours' children were in the garden at 8am doing family exercise. Then they practised their instru-ments at 9am and did schoolwork for several hours after this. In the afternoon, they went off on family cycle rides and came back and ate their vegetables at teatime. No doubt organic. I find it impossible to get my son out of bed to do any schoolwork at all and he says he hates his life. I feel I am failing completely, and I am exhausted too. I can't help it. I'm incredibly jealous.'

You are not alone: Jane's story

'Just talking about jealousy is painful. It taps into a part of me that wants what other people have: their obedient clever children; their big tidy houses; their exotic holidays and charmed work lives. As I speak this, it is of course ludicrous. There's a good German word for it: "Schadenfreude" is the experience of pleasure, joy or self-satisfaction that comes from learning of or witnessing the troubles, failure, or humiliation of another. I feel guilty and ashamed to admit that I feel that way when someone's perfect (often public) life goes tits up in some way.

'Sometimes, I think there is no hope for me given how much I compare, judge, assess and reassess all the time. How much I want more, and what other people have. But I have realised that there are some things that I can do to reduce my jealousy and to try to think differently about my situation. I truly believe that I have had experiences and feelings that are so extreme and intense that I am changed. I have learned to be more compassionate myself, less judgemental. I have met a range of people in real life or online who have given me hope and inspiration. I am in awe of how others cope in situations that ARE worse than mine.

'So, this is in some ways about reframing. There will always be people who have more than me (in good fortune, privilege, health, happy children, whatever) and there will always be people with less.'

Some of the techniques described earlier can help with jealousy and Jane's use of 'reframing' illustrates that. It may also be helpful to remember that envy is a normal emotion. It's not just found in humans either. A classic experiment showed that monkeys get envious too (and a brief video will show you envy in action). One monkey gets a piece of cucumber as a reward for performing a task and appears content with that. However, when the monkey sees another monkey receive a grape (the monkey equivalent of choco-late), then the first monkey becomes furious. If you can take a look at this video, it is really striking as well as humorous (https://youtu.be/meiU6TxysCg).

Accepting that it is normal to feel such envy, and concentrating on strategies such as focusing on the positive and writing gratitude journals can also be helpful. With a gratitude journal, as well as writing down the details of small events and actions that have hap-pened (e.g., my daughter said 'thank you'), it can also be helpful to write down the bad things that didn't happen (e.g., my daughter didn't make a fuss when I asked her to say 'hello' to a visitor).

Exercise 14.1: Gratitude journal

Today I am grateful for the following that happened:

....

....

....

Today I am grateful for the following that did not happen:

....

....

....

CHAPTER 14: SUMMARY AND KEY MESSAGES

- Anger, jealousy and envy are all normal emotions

- Identifying emotions is the first step to changing them

- Techniques such as STOPP can be helpful as well as writing a gratitude journal

---

SECTION 3:
OVERVIEW SUMMARY AND KEY MESSAGES

These chapters covered a lot of material. Ways to try to identify your emotions and increase your ability to be patient even under the most trying of circumstances were described. A key part of that was using emotion regulation strategies. Ways of thinking to try to help with your interpretation of the situation were presented, and the idea of 'cognitive errors' were introduced. Stress and coping was described with the idea of a 'stress bucket' and healthy vs. unhealthy ways of coping. Because ruminating is so unhelpful, we suggested ways to ask 'how' questions instead of 'why' questions and also addressed some potentially unhelpful behaviours that you may be doing in terms of multitasking. Treating yourself with empathy and compassion was emphasised and ways of addressing unhelpful emotions such as guilt, shame and embarrassment were provided. The chapter on responsibility will hopefully help you see that there are others to share the burden. The final chapter on jealousy and anger is included to help show that such emotions are to be expected, even if they are undesirable. Together, the key message from the chapters is that there are strategies to help you cope. These strategies are based on changing how you are thinking, feeling and behaving given the challenges of situations that you may not be able to change.

SECTION 4:
IT WORKED FOR ME – TOP TIPS FROM PEOPLE WHO HAVE BEEN THROUGH IT

15: 'Small pleasures' – things that can distract/ refocus/reframe

There is little dispute that breaking down enjoyable things into small bite-sized pieces is more sensible and realistic than it being all or nothing. Noticing the blossom, listening to the birds, enjoying a bit of nature and getting some fresh air for fifteen minutes will be beneficial nevertheless and, for many, is the only practical option.

There are two things that are important. One is giving yourself time and permission to take a moment 'out' and the other is to find things that will bring you small pleasures.

We spoke with many parents about what helped them when their children were sad, and this chapter contains the answers that came up the most. What sounds easy, for example listening to a favourite song on your headphones, can actually be very hard to do – even if headphones are easily to hand. It is also the case that for some people, they feel as though they don't deserve any pleasure. You may be so worn down caring for your child and getting through your day-to-day life that the very idea of any pleasure sounds insane.

But small pleasures are a very good place to start. Taking a moment to consciously enjoy the smallest of moments or experiences is a way of starting to 'reframe' and will help both you and your child.

Getting out and seeing friends is one of the first things people tell you to do when you are feeling sad. Obviously, this a nice thing to do in happy times and can represent normal adult life. However, it can be the most impossible of tasks if your child is unhappy and everyone else seems to be enjoying life as 'normal'. Having unhappy children is socially tough and your friendships, as well as those of your child, may have suffered.

If you or your child struggle with forming friendships in any case, then hearing about everyone else getting out and seeing friends can sound alien and unhelpful. There are many ways of finding small pleasures that are not social and can be enjoyed alone.

You are not alone: Jane's story

'On one occasion, when my son was at the height of school refusal and anguish, I attended a funeral. It was very sad. A death out of time; a young mother who had died of cancer. I had worked with her husband in my twenties (BC – Before Children) and attended the funeral with a group of my former work colleagues. It turned out to be an incredibly uplifting day. I took two trains to get there. I had a long day away from home. I met up with people I hadn't seen for years and I remembered who I had been before becoming a parent. There was lots of laughter amid the tears. I returned home feeling I had been out in the world for the first time in ages and was energised by the experience. I doubt I would have accepted a wedding invitation had one come about at that time. But a funeral was different, it came with different social expectations and unwittingly pushed me outside my comfort zone and into the kind of social situation I had been avoiding for years.'

What people have told us helps them

We have tried to group the very wide range of activities that people do that bring them comfort, help and hope. They overlap – going for a walk with a friend can be considered as being social, as doing a hobby/activity and also as getting you out into nature. There are websites that list various activities if it is hard for you to think of one that would suit your situation and we produce a very long list later in the chapter, but these are the some that parents told us that they found useful.

Social	Hobbies/ activities	Nature
• Coffee & cake with sister who also has a child with difficulties • Choir • Cinema with a friend • Talking on the phone while ironing • Going for a walk with a friend • Swapping recipes • Doing the food shop with a neighbour • Going to a comedy club	• Singing • Art • Baking • Cooking • Cleaning • Exercise • Yoga • Meditation • Sport (watching and playing) • Fishing • Reading	• Gardening • Dog walking • Walking • Open-air swimming • Taking photos of sunsets • Bird watching • Noticing the birds singing at dawn • Smelling flowers • Hearing the rain

---

You are not alone: Liane's story

'I used to sing in church as a child but haven't done any singing for ages and we don't go to church as a family anymore. But I have recently joined an online choir and it's amazing how uninhibited I have found this forum. I can keep myself off video as well, which helped with confidence initially. Something about singing, opening the throat and repeating choruses and learning lyrics feels healthy and opens me up inside.'

Liane's story is consistent with many other people's experiences. The strong emotions generated by singing are well documented. But for Ann, after the death of her daughter, her choir practice became too difficult, illustrating again that one size does not fit all.

You are not alone: Kay's story

'The feeling that I could nurture something successfully and make it grow was profound at times. When I had Kit, I hadn't really wanted children and I doubted my ability to nurture a person. Through gardening, I can see tenderness, patience and positive outcomes, in a way I can take satisfaction from. I also see results seasonally and quite quickly. It's a cliché but watching the circle of life and being connected to the seasons through seeds and plants and my garden, well, it gives me some perspective and something to hang my brain onto at times. Also, there is hope – green shoots after winter. When I see good things or changes happen with Kit it's possible to find parallels in the cycle of the natural world that make me feel positive and good.'

You are not alone: Nimmi's story

'Cooking. Mending something. Cleaning difficult things – a little corner I've made better. I have a cleaning gene – everyone will have something comparable to that. I often think I must be a very superficial person that I do that, but it's a distraction and enjoyable so I relish it.'

You are not alone: Alana's story

'Yoga practice is great; everything about it makes me wonder why I don't do it every day. But actually, getting to a class is often very hard to manage and I am lucky if I make it there once a week with any regularity. Since lockdown, I have discovered the joys of free online yoga. This doesn't mean I am doing it every day, but I am finding short sessions (fifteen minutes as opposed to an hour-long class) that I can do at home and have even involved my son on occasions. He likes the ritual (getting out a mat, ninja warrior poses) and of course I love the fact that we are doing something together and he's not hunched over a computer screen for that brief moment of the day.'

You are not alone: Jane's story

'Piano – the discipline of scales, the mental concentration of picking out the notes on a new piece, all provided distraction and helped me not to think, which at times was a blessed relief. I also have two jam jars in the kitchen that

> *I try and fill with flowers or sprigs of leaves, dried grasses, depending on the season. It's all a bit home-maker/Little House on the Prairie, but actually cutting and choosing seasonal plants and arranging them quickly and putting them on the table gives me a moment of control and joy. It's a small enough canvas to work with and gives me a good pleasure/activity ratio. Sometimes I photo them on my phone, but I haven't got round to working out how to do Instagram yet, and probably never will.'*

For some people, it can be helpful to think about what they used to do before they had children. Jane's story of attending a funeral reminded her of the person that she used to be. The same was true for Matteo, who remembered the pleasure he got from art.

You are not alone: Matteo's story

'I used to love drawing and colouring in as a child. I loved looking at the pencil colours in art shops and learning the names of paints. A while ago, I bought myself a packet of blank postcards and sometimes I take five minutes to doodle on them; flowers, fish, trees, birds, whatever comes to mind. Simple, basic images appeal to me. But I like the pause they represent, and they give me a mini sense of satisfaction. I use the children's coloured pencils, though I suppose I could get my own.'

Pet ownership

Ah, getting a dog. Not exactly a small pleasure; could be a very large one, or not a pleasure at all if it doesn't go well.

Walks and walking the dog featured largely in our conversations. Many parents with unhappy children become dog converts along the way, if money, space and time allow. The basic love and enthusiasm generated by the family dog (less so by the family cat) can be a healthy step-change for the whole family. This obviously comes with provisos. Taking on a dog is costly, time-consuming, life-changing and probably not that good for the planet. It's another mouth to feed and another being to be responsible for. I can see why many parents baulk at the prospect.

However, if the gamble pays off, there is exercise, friendship and unconditional love from another source. An additional heartbeat in the home that provides less complexity and usually comes with an easier training manual than with all the others. Dogs don't solve problems, but they can provide distraction and focus for every person in the household. Pets as therapy are in so many places and give so much pleasure – prisons, schools, hospices, mental health units, etc., and the home is no different.

You are not alone: Sai's story

'I never wanted a dog. When we agreed this was a route to consider, I did tonnes of research and ended up with a small dog, as I realised I would end up doing most of the work. It was astonishing how the dog helped Greg in social situations. We would be out walking, and someone would come and coo over the puppy. Instead of being awkward and embarrassed, he would be able to have a conversation about the puppy. It acted like a lightning rod/conduit of sorts and took away some of the embarrassment that social interaction had held.

'It also helped me. I remember one morning taking the puppy out for a wee on the lawn at 3am, and watching a huge moon rising and getting an overwhelming sense of life force, for the first time in years. Something about the puppy's immediate needs and the ease of the emotional connection, waggy tail, unconditional love and need, the peace of it being non-verbal, just threw a switch in me. I began to feel hopeful and lighter. It was definitely a turning point for me.'

Practical hobbies

For some, it just isn't practical to have a pet, or the thought of yet another responsibility has zero appeal. Trying to find pleasures when all your time may be taken up with caring or work or other children is a major challenge. Some practical ideas from other parents such as Jaime may be helpful.

You are not alone: Jaime's experience

'We were so often in waiting rooms waiting for appointments and specialists that I began keeping a pack of playing cards in my bag. If I was on my own, I would clear the table of magazines and set up patience. If we were together, we would sometimes play card games and it would be a mini distraction in a stressful place at a stressful time.'

Sometimes communicating to your partner or others the importance of your hobbies may be important, as in Alex's situation.

You are not alone: Alex's experience

*'Supporting a team, I watch sport. I know it really p****s everyone else off at times. I am a massive football fan and since Finn has been ill, it has become more extreme. I am utterly obsessed with my team. But it gives me moments of real involvement and pleasure. I probably need to find a way of articulating this to everyone else, so they don't think I just don't care about what's going on at home.'*

Some parents we spoke to gave us examples of how helpful it was for them to keep learning. Mastering a new skill or finding out a new fact that would stretch their brain, for example by doing crossword or Sudoku puzzles, gave them mini moments of concentration and release. Other people found writing particularly helpful.

You are not alone: Mo's experience

'When my daughter was very ill, I did an MA in creative writing. I was very conscious it was something for me, to build up myself. I made sentences about the world in my head. It was essential to me, in shaping my experience into something tangible and communicable.'

When struggling with a child who cannot cope, it is very easy to lose yourself. Your personality, your likes and dislikes. You are in survival mode. Sometimes, humour can be particularly helpful in managing the dark times.

> ## You are not alone: Kat's experience
>
> *'I used to be a funny person, but my daily life meant that it was hard to find things funny in the same way. But I kept on watching my favourite comedy shows and, to my surprise, I sometimes found myself laughing through my tears. I felt better after watching them, and when I retold sections from them to other people, I found I enjoyed making other people laugh too. Since then, I have made a conscious effort to use humour wherever I can – it helps me manage.'*

Short vs. long term

It is clear that people are very different, and what they find helpful is also very different. Some of the activities in this section will bring comfort, help and hope immediately, for example seeing someone for coffee. However, other strategies may be longer term, for example trying to get fitter.

Exercise 15.1: Identifying your small pleasures

Use the list of pleasurable activities on the next few pages (reproduced with permission from the information sheet: Fun Activities Catalogue, health.wa.gov.au), or the descriptions from other people earlier in this chapter to think about some things that bring you small pleasures. Some of the activities may not be practical. However, some are much easier to do (smelling a flower, whistling). You can also think about some things that you used to do that you no longer do. Identify one or two that are practical for you to start doing. Once you have done them, reflect on whether they were helpful or whether there may be other ones for you to try.

FUN ACTIVITIES CATALOGUE

The following is a list of activities that might be fun and pleasurable for you. Feel free to add your own fun activities to the list

1. Going to a quiz or trivia night
2. Spending time in nature
3. Watching the clouds drift by
4. Debating
5. Painting my nails
6. Going ice skating, roller skating/blading
7. Scheduling a day with nothing to do
8. Giving positive feedback about something (e.g. writing a letter or email about good service)
9. Feeding the birds
10. Spending an evening with good friends
11. Making jams or preserves
12. Going out to dinner
13. Buying gifts
14. Having a political discussion
15. Repairing things around the house
16. Washing my car
17. Watching TV, videos
18. Sending a loved one a card in the mail
19. Baking something to share with others (e.g. family, neighbours, friends, work colleagues)
20. Taking a sauna, spa or a steam bath
21. Having a video call with someone who lives far away
22. Organising my wardrobe
23. Playing musical instruments
24. Going to the ballet or opera
25. Lighting scented candles, oils or incense
26. Spending time alone
27. Exercising
28. Putting up a framed picture or artwork
29. Flirting
30. Entertaining
31. Riding a motorbike
32. Wine tasting
33. Going to the planetarium or observatory
34. Birdwatching
35. Doing something spontaneously
36. Going on a picnic
37. Having a warm drink
38. Massaging hand cream into my hands
39. Fantasising about the future
40. Laughing
41. Flying a plane
42. Playing tennis or badminton
43. Clearing my email inbox
44. Planting a terrarium
45. Playing lawn games (e.g. bowls, croquet, bocce)
46. Going to a party
47. Getting out of debt/paying debts
48. Seeing and/or showing photos

49. Going on a city tour
50. Going to an agricultural show
51. Jogging, walking
52. Going to open houses
53. Researching a topic of interest
54. Going to the beach
55. Redecorating
56. Volunteering for a cause I support
57. Smelling a flower
58. Opening the curtains and blinds to let light in
59. Going to the zoo or aquarium
60. Doing jigsaw puzzles
61. Donating old clothes or items to charity
62. Lying in the sun
63. Learning a magic trick
64. Talking on the phone
65. Listening to a podcast or radio show
66. Walking around my city and noticing architecture of buildings
67. Doing arts and crafts
68. Going on a ghost tour
69. Sketching, painting
70. Mowing the lawn
71. Going horseback riding
72. Doing the dishes
73. Sitting outside and listening to birds sing
74. Going to a free public lecture
75. Travelling to national parks
76. Going to a fair or fete
77. Playing cards
78. Putting moisturising cream on my face / body
79. Volunteering at an animal shelter
80. Re-watching a favourite movie
81. Gardening
82. Going camping
83. Playing volleyball
84. Going bike riding
85. Entering a competition
86. Doing crossword puzzles
87. Patting or cuddling my pet
88. Cooking a special meal
89. Soaking in the bathtub
90. Having a treatment at a day spa (e.g. facial)
91. Putting extra effort in to my appearance
92. Playing golf
93. Doing a favour for someone
94. Building a bird house or feeder
95. Looking at pictures of beautiful scenery
96. Having family get-togethers
97. Listening to music
98. Learning a new language
99. Taking a free online class
100. Working
101. Washing my hair
102. Singing around the house
103. Flipping through old photo albums
104. Upcycling or creatively reusing old items
105. Going sailing
106. Stretching muscles
107. Maintaining a musical instrument (e.g. restringing guitar)
108. Playing soccer

15: 'Small pleasures' – things that can distract/refocus/reframe

109. Buying clothes
110. Going to the botanic gardens
111. Going to a scenic spot and enjoying the view
112. Going to the speedway
113. Snuggling up with a soft blanket
114. Listening to an audiobook
115. Going to see live stand-up comedy
116. Writing down a list of things I am grateful for
117. Maintaining an aquarium
118. Playing Frisbee
119. Teaching a special skill to someone else (e.g. knitting, woodworking, painting, language)
120. Playing chess (with a friend or at a local club)
121. Going to a games arcade
122. Jumping on a trampoline
123. Sending a text message to a friend
124. Going fishing
125. Doodling
126. Putting a vase of fresh flowers in my house
127. Participating in a protest I support
128. Going to a movie
129. Surfing, bodyboarding or stand up paddle boarding
130. Baking home-made bread
131. Walking barefoot on soft grass
132. Watching a movie marathon
133. Skipping/ jumping rope
134. Being physically intimate with someone I want to be close to
135. Going to karaoke
136. Wearing an outfit that makes me feel good
137. Cooking some meals to freeze for later
138. Hobbies (stamp collecting, model building, etc.)
139. Talking to an older relative and asking them questions about their life
140. Listening to classical music
141. Photography
142. Watching funny videos on YouTube
143. Doing something religious or spiritual (e.g. going to church, praying)
144. Seeing a movie at the drive-in or outdoor cinema
145. Making my bed with fresh sheets
146. Lifting weights
147. Early morning coffee and newspaper
148. Planning a themed party (e.g. costume, murder mystery)
149. Wearing comfortable clothes
150. Shining my shoes
151. Acting
152. Going swimming
153. De-cluttering
154. Going rock climbing
155. Whittling
156. Going on a ride at a theme park or fair
157. Arranging flowers
158. Going to the gym
159. Working on my car or bicycle
160. Juggling or learning to juggle

161. Contacting an old school friend
162. Calligraphy
163. Sleeping
164. Driving
165. Going crabbing
166. Playing with my pets
167. Abseiling
168. Going kayaking, canoeing or white-water rafting
169. Listening to the radio
170. Doing Sudoku
171. Planting vegetables or flowers
172. Walking on the riverfront/ foreshore
173. Shooting pool or playing billiards
174. Getting an indoor plant
175. Surfing the internet
176. Doing embroidery, cross stitching
177. Browsing a hardware store
178. Donating blood
179. Buying books
180. Meditating
181. Training my pet to do a new trick
182. Planning a day's activities
183. Waking up early, and getting ready at a leisurely pace
184. Going to a Bingo night
185. Playing ping pong / table tennis
186. Buying an ice-cream from an ice-cream truck
187. Going on a hot air balloon ride
188. Sightseeing
189. Organising my work space
190. Dangling my feet off a jetty
191. Writing (e.g. poems, articles, blog, books)
192. Dancing in the dark
193. Having an indoor picnic
194. Reading classic literature
195. Going on a date
196. Taking children places
197. Going whale watching
198. Putting on perfume or cologne
199. Digging my toes in the sand
200. Hitting golf balls at a driving range
201. Reading magazines or newspapers
202. Calling a friend
203. Sending a handwritten letter
204. Going snorkelling
205. Going hiking, bush walking
206. Reading fiction
207. Meeting new people
208. Doing 5 minutes of calm deep breathing
209. Buying new stationary
210. Turning off electronic devices for an hour (e.g. computer, phone, TV)
211. Buying music (MP3s, CDs, records)
212. Relaxing
213. Going to a footy game (or rugby, soccer, basketball, etc.)
214. Going skiing
215. Doing woodworking
216. Planning a nice surprise for someone else
217. Playing video games
218. Holding a garage sale

15: 'Small pleasures' – things that can distract/refocus/reframe

219. Saying 'I love you'
220. Making a playlist of upbeat songs
221. Colouring in
222. Playing laser tag or paintball
223. Joining a community choir
224. Doing a nagging task (e.g. making a phone call, scheduling an appointment, replying to an email)
225. Taking a ferry ride
226. Shaping a bonsai plant
227. Watching planes take off/ land at the airport
228. Planning my career
229. Reading non-fiction
230. Writing a song or composing music
231. Taking my dog to the park
232. Borrowing books from the library
233. Having a barbecue
234. Sewing
235. Dancing
236. Having lunch with a friend
237. Talking to or introducing myself to my neighbours
238. Holding hands
239. Going to a free art exhibition
240. Making a 'To-Do' list of tasks
241. Travelling abroad, interstate or within the state
242. Having quiet evenings
243. Geocaching
244. Singing in the shower
245. Browsing at a second hand book shop
246. Test driving an expensive car
247. Refurbishing furniture
248. Exchanging emails, chatting on the internet
249. Knitting/crocheting/quilting
250. Napping in a hammock
251. Skipping stones on the water
252. Doing ballet, jazz/tap dancing
253. Archery
254. Going on a Segway tour
255. Visiting a grandparent
256. Making a gift for someone
257. Having discussions with friends
258. Trying a new recipe
259. Pampering myself at home (e.g. putting on a face mask)
260. Watching my children play
261. Going to a community or school play
262. Making jewellery
263. Reading poetry
264. Going to the hills
265. Getting/giving a massage
266. Shooting hoops at the local basketball courts
267. Flying kites
268. Savouring a piece of fresh fruit
269. Playing hockey
270. Eating outside during my lunch break
271. Floating on a pool lounge
272. Making a pot of tea
273. Using special items (e.g. fine china, silver cutlery, jewellery, clothes, souvenir mugs)
274. Doing a DIY project (e.g. making homemade soap, making a mosaic)

275. Taking care of my plants
276. Telling a joke
277. Going to a public place and people watching
278. Discussing books
279. Going window shopping
280. Watching boxing, wrestling
281. Giving someone a genuine compliment
282. Practising yoga, Pilates
283. Walking around the block
284. Shaving
285. Genuinely listening to others
286. Participating in a clean-up (e.g. picking up litter at the beach or park)
287. Eating fish and chips at the beach
288. Rearranging the furniture in my house
289. Doing water aerobics
290. Blowing bubbles
291. Buying new furniture
292. Watching a sunset or sunrise
293. Star gazing
294. Watching a funny TV show or movie
295. Making pottery, or taking a pottery class
296. Playing mini golf
297. Recycling old items
298. Going to a water park
299. Practising karate, judo
300. Boxing a punching bag
301. Cleaning
302. Driving a Go Kart
303. Daydreaming
304. Learning about my family tree
305. Picking berries at a farm
306. Watching kids play sport
307. Setting up a budget
308. Writing a positive comment on a website /blog
309. Getting a manicure or pedicure
310. Collecting things (coins, shells, etc.)
311. Playing cricket
312. Signing up for a fun run
313. Scrapbooking
314. Accepting an invitation
315. Cooking an international cuisine
316. Solving riddles
317. Scuba diving
318. Watching home videos
319. Building a sand castle
320. Planning a holiday
321. Sitting at the beach or river and watching the movement of the water
322. Watching fireworks
323. Making home-made pizza
324. Cheering for a sports team
325. Origami
326. Doing something nostalgic (e.g. eating a childhood treat, listening to music from a certain time in my life)
327. Joining a club (e.g. film, book, sewing, etc.)
328. Lighting candles
329. Going bowling
330. Going to museums, art galleries
331. Reading comics
332. Having coffee at a cafe
333. Trying new hairstyles
334. Taking a road trip

15: 'Small pleasures' – things that can distract/refocus/reframe

335. Watching a fireplace or campfire
336. Whistling
337. Playing darts
338. Going to a flea market
339. Working from home
340. Buying a meal from a food truck or hawkers market and eating outdoors
341. Operating a remote control car / plane
342. Playing board games (e.g. Scrabble, Monopoly)
343. Savouring a piece of chocolate
344. Hunting for a bargain at an op shop, garage sale or auction
345. Buying, selling stocks and shares
346. Going to plays and concerts
347. Buying fresh food at the market
348. Beachcombing
349. Dining out at a restaurant or café
350. Harvesting home grown produce
351. Exploring with a metal detector
352. Giving someone a hug
353. Taking a holiday
354. Going to the hairdresser or barber
355. Swimming with dolphins
356. Picking flowers
357. Sandboarding
358. Going to the beauty salon
359. Buying myself something nice

360. Playing squash
361. Eating something nourishing (e.g. chicken soup)
362. Babysitting for someone
363. Taking a class (e.g. cooking, improvisation, acting, art)
364. Combing or brushing my hair
365. Writing diary/journal entries

Others:

| |
| |
| |
| |
| |
| |
| |
| |
| |
| |
| |
| |
| |
| |
| |
| |

CHAPTER 15: SUMMARY AND KEY MESSAGES

- Trying to have small pleasures in your life can be very helpful

- Different pleasures/activities will suit different people

16: Try this at home – some helpful strategies and personal strengths

The people we spoke to described how they had found other strategies to be helpful, and that they had found a personal strength to help them get through the day.

What worked for me: Karoline's story

'I am a different person at work, so I just tried to go into "work mode". I tried to think of myself as a customer on a helpdesk. I used Gantt Charts and Project Management software to try to set goals for myself and my family. We created a ritual and routine for the entire family and had a "talking stick" so that only the person holding the stick could talk. We later changed the "talking stick" to a stress ball as that seemed to work better.'

What worked for me: Renee's story

'I joined a parent support group. I found that having a network of parents in a similar position gave me both an insider's

perspective but also an outsider's – outside my family but inside the big family of parents struggling with the same problems. I found that it pays to be honest – to people we don't particularly know well. We assume we are honest with family and friends, although I am sure that can be disputed at every level! But sometimes trusting a stranger, or someone who doesn't know you well, with details of your struggles, can pay off dramatically. Someone who can see the situation from a distance and with clarity, with no emotional buy-in themselves. This also helps us feel part of a universal struggle, which has the potential to take away some of the personal loneliness of it all.'

What worked for me: Pera's story

'My partner and I tended to yell at each other and dis-agree on lots of things. We decided to focus parentally on what we could do together, rather than snipe, blame each other and be divisive (so easy). We used some self-help books on parenting to help us work together as a team.'

What worked for me: Cory's story

'I used humour and making up funny stories about the lives of people. I did it for me, to get me through it, but it also helped me bond with my daughter.'

What worked for me: Abiyana's story

'I just decided to be spontaneous and, once a week, I would say "yes" to something rather than "no".'

What worked for me: Sophia's story

'Everyone is so solution-focused, but I felt that we had been down that route and it just impacted my relationship with my daughter and frustrated her. So, I decided to try something different. I decided to just shut up (hard for me). I just sat with her pain, waiting for it to pass. In doing that, I found it calmed me too. My pain passed with hers.'

What worked for me: Chris's story

'This might sound ridiculous, but I really like those brief videos that come up about animals being rescued and having a happy ending. A sort of real-world Disney. I found looking at those gave me hope that there can be happy endings. Looking at cute pictures, sharing memes, piglets, ducklings. Holding onto cuteness and playfulness got me through the bleakest times and I think it helped my son as well.'

What worked for me: Daphne's story

'I found writing helped a lot. Writing a journal, writing how I was feeling, writing down what beautiful things I noticed, keeping a combination of a "gratitude/positives" journal so listing at the end of each day what I was grateful for, what was positive. Sometimes it was the smallest of things – like I had fresh milk for my cup of tea. But writing it down really helped me notice these things, helped me see any change, and gave me hope by reminding me that "this too will pass". Nothing is forever. And there are usually some positives to be found – even if it takes a while to think of them and they're pretty small.'

What worked for me: Alicia's story

'There's been a lot of stuff about kindness being a good idea. So, I decided I would try to be kind for a day. Or really, just try to do one kind thing. I had a voucher for the store that I wasn't using so I gave it to the woman behind me in the queue. She could use that voucher and although it wasn't very much, she was really grateful, and it made me feel like a good person (despite the awfulness going on at home). I got the bug. The next time I was at the store, I could see someone didn't have a coin for the trolley, so I gave them mine for free. It was pouring with rain and the woman thanked me so much like she had won the lottery. I just try to do one kind thing a week and find that helpful.'

What worked for me: Vikram's story

'I would say what gave me most help and hope was living in the present. The past can't be changed and the future is unknown, so just taking it day by day, even hour by hour was probably the best advice I was ever given. The same thing applies to tasks – I just break them down so they are smaller and more manageable.'

What worked for me: Usaya's story

'I recognised I was struggling to cope, so went to get some professional support for myself. Doing that was the best thing ever because it helped me understand my role in the family situation without making me feel as if I was to blame. We talked about my childhood, my issues and my own struggles. I realised that I had some autistic traits as well as my child and that really released me from a lot of guilt.'

What worked for me: Roxana's story

'I am not religious, but during a recent phase of waking up early and worrying and going over things again and again in my head, I spoke to a wise trustee at work and we just happened to start talking about the big stuff. He is extremely spiritual in the broadest sense of the word and has been through many life-changing experiences.

As a result, he has come through with a bit of an aura around him. I told him how difficult my home life was at the moment, with a few details. He suggested prayer, and my initial reaction was to shut down completely. He must have sensed this in me because he persisted. Just put it out there, he said. Reframe the things you are worrying about. Phrase them in a hopeful way, instead of catastrophising. Ask for help. So, for a while now, I have been lying in bed at 5am wrenching my brain away from disaster-mode and into something else.'

What worked for me: Laura's story

'I don't believe in God, so my appeal is to the universe – it works better for me. I appeal for help in finding the strength within me to understand and appreciate my daughter better. If I can start to consciously love and appreciate her more, that can only be a good thing for both of us.'

What worked for me: Viki's story

'I know you want to know things that helped me, but it's very hard to separate that from strategies to help the family more generally. For example, when we were trying to get the children to behave we had a pasta jar. Every time they were "good", we would put a piece of pasta in and when the jar was full, we had a treat as a family. We were fairly generous with the pasta pieces and would fill

up the jar pretty quickly, as keeping the positive momen-
tum going was part of the plan. Since family life has now
changed, we try and play a different game. On the rare
occasions I manage to get us round the table for a meal,
we do "gratitudes". Say something we are grateful for and
put a piece of pasta in the jar. It can be really small things
and they can repeat daily. It's not a competition or something to catch anyone out. It's just an attempt to focus on
the things we do have in our lives that are going well or we
enjoy. Recent inputs include "It's not raining today", "the
cat stayed on my bed all night" and "hot water". We all
remember the boiler breaking last autumn. "Not getting
divorced yet" has also featured. This can be solitary or
family-focused depending on what the current dynamics
might be. Not always easy but part of the process is to put
a leveller down. Getting back to elemental human basics
such as food, warmth and shelter. Which are easy to forget
when Netflix is refusing to load.'

Exercise 16.1: Reflecting on your own strengths

Looking back on your experiences, what would you say has
helped you the most?

....

....

....

....

What advice would you give to others (or yourself)?

....

....

....

....

Of all the stories above, which one do you think has relevance for you and might you try in the future?

....

....

....

....

CHAPTER 16: SUMMARY AND KEY MESSAGES

- Parents have very different ways to help them manage

- Some people write, others set up support groups and others try to take each day as it comes

- Identifying your own strengths and finding what strategies work for you can provide help and hope in difficult times

- This can be summarised by the quote 'You are stronger than you think'

17: Comfort, help and hope in a nutshell

Many families told us that mantras and memes were important in providing comfort, help and hope. Why are mantras helpful? What do they do? It seems that they serve to focus the brain and give us something to hang onto at very hard times. They can help gather difficult thoughts, keep a sense of perspective, company and hope. Some of the mantras and quotes families told us about are below.

'You are doing the best you can at this time'

'If you lie on a rock for long enough you get used to it!'

'She will get there in the end'

'I set a very low bar'

'Make it a rule of life never to regret and never to look back. Regret is an appalling waste of energy; you can't build on it it's only good for wallowing in' (Katherine Mansfield)

'Often regret is very false and displaced, and imagines the past to be totally other than it was' (John O'Donohue)

'The past is a foreign country; they do things differently there' (L. P. Hartley)

'There's a world of difference between truth and facts. Facts can obscure the truth' (Maya Angelou)

'If I am not good to myself, how can I expect anyone else to be good to me?' (Maya Angelou)

'When you can do nothing, what can you do?' (Buddhist koan)

'Smile, breathe and go slowly' (Thich Nhat Hanh)

'Don't just do something; stand there!' (Martin Gabel)

'One does not become fully human painlessly' (Rollo May)

'The cure for pain is in the pain' (Rumi)

Action for Happiness (www.actionforhappiness.org) have a useful set of posters that can serve as a quick boost and reminder of some of the strategies to help when times are tough. Three key ones are below:

17: Comfort, help and hope in a nutshell

Other bite-size memorable sayings that can be helpful are:

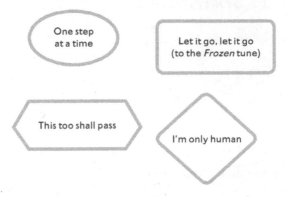

One step
at a time

Let it go, let it go
(to the *Frozen* tune)

This too shall pass

I'm only human

Exercise 17.1: Phrases to help you through

Use the blank space below to write down any brief sayings/
phrases that you find help you get through the tough moments.

CHAPTER 17: SUMMARY AND KEY MESSAGES

- Brief sayings, images or phrases from songs can be powerful ways to help manage in the moment

- Such sayings also emphasise that many other people have shared the same experiences

SECTION 4:
OVERVIEW SUMMARY AND KEY MESSAGES

This section describes how other people have managed during their most challenging times. It is clear that such methods are highly personal. We all have a different idea of what distracts us, what gives us pleasure, and what we find helpful. Some of the strategies might work at one point in time for one situation, but then seem to lose their effect. Many of us would credit our pets with helping us get through the tough times, yet others would see pet ownership as an additional burdensome responsibility. The very long list of activities means we hope there will be something that you can find that will be helpful. Finding the time to do them can be challenging and it may mean you just opt for a nutshell saying on your phone. We hope these tips, together with the more formal strategies supported by research, will bring you comfort and be useful during the tough times.

SECTION 5: ACCEPTANCE

18: Acceptance

How could 'acceptance' have any relevance to a world where your child is struggling to cope? How on Earth can that ever be 'acceptable'?

We hope that some of the strategies in Sections 1 to 4 have given you lots of helpful ideas about things you might try to help you cope when your child can't. We hope that these illustrate to you that you are far from powerless – you can make changes which can make things feel better. However, as well as this – and, for some, at the heart of it all – we think it's important to practise acceptance.

Sometimes, despite our very best efforts, and despite the agonising desire to alleviate our kids' (and our own) pain, there are problems we can't solve. If you're reading this book, it's likely you can think of some right now. We can.

We can't take away their physical illnesses. We can't make them look any different or run faster. We can't make friends for them. We can't undo their pasts – where they were born; the schools they went to; the things we or others said to them; what they consumed; their genetic inheritance; the drugs they took; what they saw; accidents they were involved in. There's so much which is simply beyond our control. And sometimes, there's just no choice but to 'live with it'. But how?

What we definitely *don't* mean here is what's often meant when someone says flippantly, 'just live with it'. Neither 'acceptance' nor 'just living with it' make any sense if they mean being passive or just giving up. Acceptance is not giving up. We choose to think of acceptance as an active state, that we come to by engaging with the reality of our child's problems in a way that also accepts our own need to survive, and even, maybe, to thrive. It means daring to accept what is, now, and it can be transformative.

The meaning of 'acceptance' that we will work towards in this chapter is not just a blanket acceptance of a situation, although sometimes that might also come into it. So, we don't mean accepting that your child 'has depression', or is lonely, scared or ill, because none of those things is simple and constant and defined by a single label, especially as it affects your unique child. Accepting what is, now, is like loosening the strings around that package of problems and taking a look and seeing what's really in there. You may recognise how easy it is to get tangled up in desperate arguments with yourself, going over the same questions, as described in Chapter 8. Arguments about how you could have improved things; about everything your mind says you've done wrong; about how terribly things might turn out; about how things ought to be, and why they're not. We think acceptance is to do with stepping out of that tangle of thinking. It's existing meaningfully, and maybe even thriving, right in the eye of the storm. It's letting yourself feel what you are feeling. It's about stopping *trying* to be, or feel, or not feel, anything in particular.

What are we accepting?

'Accept the things you cannot change . . . '

Alcoholics Anonymous adopted what's known as The Serenity Prayer (originally written by Reinhart Niebuhr, a twentieth-century theologian): 'God grant me the serenity to accept the things I cannot change, courage to change the things I can, and wisdom to know the difference.' You may know it. Other people have expressed similar thoughts, without necessarily involving God. Maya Angelou said: 'If you don't like something, change it. If you can't change it, change your attitude', while B. K. S. Iyengar, founder of Iyengar Yoga, said 'Yoga teaches us to cure what need not be endured and endure what cannot be cured.'

Sounds sensible, doesn't it? But what does it look like to recognise and 'accept' the things we can't change? It's often not even easy to tell which things they are. Unfortunately, even when we do see logically that something can't be changed, for example because it's in the past, it's not always easy to feel that we can 'accept' it.

You are not alone: Omar's story

'It was just before our daughter Mevish's fourteenth birthday when Nazreen (my wife) and I realised we weren't managing the way things were at home. We were afraid we couldn't keep Mevish safe, and our son was suffering too. He was only ten and he was being woken up by his sister trying to get out of the house, sometimes two, three times in the night, and getting aggressive with us when we tried to stop her. We were all exhausted. But it's a terrible decision to take – to send your child away. It's unthinkable. Residential care isn't what you ever think you could accept for your own child. Any parent who's had to do it knows how painful – agonising, really – it is.

'To even speak of it felt like betraying Mevish. That was such a terrible time, but it was necessary to recognise that her challenges needed handling by people with the

experience to help her better than we could. She has learning difficulties and autism and these problems came to a head when she reached her teens. We were just not coping, and our distress and frustration were harming both our children. Our relationship with both children was being damaged because fighting this losing battle to handle Mevish's problems, and their effects on our son, was leaving us no time or energy to just be parents.

'And so, gradually we realised that to be fair to us all was to be fair to Mevish as well, because she was suffering in so many ways. It was a terribly difficult transition – handing her over to the care of others when that was the last thing any of us could ever have wanted. I still struggle with it sometimes but at the same time I can see that it was the right thing to do. She took time to settle, but she now has bonds with people as well as us who care about her, and we can concentrate on being loving parents to her and to our son, who also is free to love his sister and live his own life with us too. The guilt we felt was hard to deal with, but we have learnt to let it go more as we've seen that the benefits for all the family are good for Mevish too. We have slowly accepted that looking after Mevish was beyond our capabilities, and that it's OK to admit that. Our stress and despair were hurting her too, but we've reached a much better point with that now. We see Mevish several times a week, and we have some really great times together, and I think we all feel supported. We're still just as much her parents, and she's still just as much our daughter.'

Some parents have spoken about wanting to accept something more than they feel they do.

You are not alone: Petra's story

Petra is a single mum of Alfie, her fifteen-year-old son. Alfie was diagnosed with Type 1 diabetes when he was eleven, after being admitted to hospital as an emergency. This was shortly after his parents divorced, after years of arguments. Petra has found the diabetes difficult to manage. Alfie has also had lots of problems with his mood and has had diagnoses of depression and anxiety. He often feels and expresses anger with his mum, whom he's said he blames for both his diabetes and the fact his dad doesn't live with them anymore. He's currently refusing to go to school, and it's difficult to get him to go to medical appointments when needed.

Petra told us:

'A lot of stuff has happened with Alfie which I wish hadn't. I've spent so long wondering why he got diabetes and beating myself up about the ways I might have caused it or contributed to it. Or working out how I could have recognised it earlier, so he could have been treated sooner. There's always something you can find on the internet about causes, to make you feel terrible, like a crap parent. I'd tell myself "He has these problems and you just have to make your peace with that", but this would never sink in.'

Like with Petra, just telling ourselves to 'accept' something often doesn't work. Luckily, there are other ways to approach this.

Accepting our own reactions

If you've picked up this book, it's probably already quite clear to you that having a child who is suffering is incredibly hard. Living with the intertwined pain of our children and ourselves can strip us bare and leave us open to the elements.

And there's no escaping that, to some extent, the range of excruciating reactions you might have – devastation, fear, confusion, exhaustion, irritation, anger – will reflect this.

There's yet *another* layer of suffering, though, that we almost all tend to superimpose on all of this. The fact is that trying to escape from these feelings (and who wouldn't want to, sometimes?) can add to your difficulties. We've spoken in earlier chapters about how we might try to 'escape' by using unhelpful coping strategies (Chapter 7). But there are more subtle ways we're all constantly trying to escape, too. Phones, the internet, TV, inescapable busyness, thinking.

And all the time we're making judgements. We judge what's going on in the world around us and our child, and we label events and situations 'good' or 'bad' for our child, for our family, for us. But as well as all that, we're constantly judging our own reactions to everything that's happening.

All the parents we spoke to were clear about how distressing it can be when your child is suffering. Some struggled with feelings of anger, jealousy and envy, but also with disliking 'that side' of themselves. The three of us have also spoken about how none of us 'likes' our tendency to compare ourselves with other people and envy them when things seem to be going 'better' with their children than with ours. It's something we talk about like a guilty secret.

You are not alone: Petra's story

'Sometimes, I've felt really livid with my friends for having it so much easier. Angry and jealous. Then I can feel guilty about that, because they've done nothing wrong. But I've

had very mean thoughts, like that I wish one of their kids had an illness, not mine.'

You are not alone: Matthew's story

'Sometimes, I just think, "Sod them all" about my children and get this feeling of independence and self-sufficiency. But then I wonder what that means about me that I think that.'

You are not alone: Jaswinder's story

'Sometimes, when my daughter would call me in the night because she was struggling, I'd get this overwhelming feeling of rage. I was just so exhausted. I really didn't want to feel angry, but I couldn't help it.'

You are not alone: Phoebe's story

'My son's behaviour was just so horrendous. He would rage, throw things, swear at me. On one level I wanted to sympathise because I knew it was because he was very upset, but I hated that behaviour so much. It made me want to cry and scream at the same time, or walk out of the house and never come back. Actually, truth be told, sometimes it made me want to punch him.'

Sometimes, other people, as well as ourselves, judge our reactions. Many of us have also experienced being told to cheer up, to see the positives, to be thankful. The sad reality is that we're existing in a world in which we're often desperate for our suffering to go away, and so are other people, because it's uncomfortable to witness. It's a tall order to be expected to see the positives and feel thankful. If we're honest, we've probably all been on both sides of this.

So, how can we find a way through it all? Well, there's a considerable amount of evidence that judging our reactions and avoiding certain thoughts and feelings can make them *more* of a problem, not less. So, in the next chapter, let's look at how we might find a way to step off this exhausting hamster wheel of negative emotions and thoughts.

CHAPTER 18: SUMMARY AND KEY MESSAGES

- There are always situations with our children which we can't change – and it can be hard to feel we 'accept' these

- Wanting to escape and avoid situations or how we're feeling about them is a very human reaction. However, trying to escape can make things more difficult in the long run

- We don't have to accept everything all at once, but accepting the present moment – including our own reactions – is something we can practise, and can be a radical and transformative step towards reducing distress

- Acceptance is an active process, and is not giving up

19: Accepting the contents of the present moment (the 'full catastrophe')

Most of us have probably encountered the term, or been advised to 'try', mindfulness at some point (maybe infuriatingly often, if only via glib social media memes). A lot of people over the centuries (from the Buddha, to Daoists in ancient China, to – more recently – speakers and writers like Jiddu Krishnamurti and Eckhart Tolle) have made similar observations about the power of paying attention to – accepting – the present moment. In the 1980s, Jon Kabat-Zinn was instrumental in bringing 'mindfulness meditation' practice to the treatment of chronic pain, in America. There's now a decent body of evidence that practising mindfulness meditation can make people with many different problems (from depression and anxiety to physical health complaints) feel better.

Used slightly differently from more passive standard definitions, 'acceptance' is one of the interconnected 'attitudes of mind' Jon Kabat-Zinn uses to describe 'mindfulness'. Mindfulness, too, is difficult to put into words (by its nature it's non-verbal), but Jon Kabat-Zinn's definition, *'the awareness that arises from paying attention, on purpose, in the present moment and non-judgementally'*, is popular. So, Kabat-Zinn says mindfulness is the awareness that develops when we practise focusing on the present moment in a non-judgemental way. That is to say that we deliberately swap making a judgement for positively choosing to accept everything that arises in that moment. And that is what we mean here by acceptance.

There's lots to debate about the issues involved in taking elements of Zen Buddhism (and other Eastern traditions) and practising them in the individualised 'Western' culture and mindsets of the writers – and we're guessing most of the readers – of this book. However, the fact remains that for many people, practising mindfulness (in one form or other) reduces suffering, and leads us out of the mental traps we can weave for ourselves. Leaving aside most of the details of specific packages (some now heavily commercialised), practice in present-moment acceptance/awareness is strongly relevant when it comes to addressing the situation at the heart of this book: your child is suffering, so you are too.

Soon after his initial experiences working with people with chronic physical pain conditions, Jon Kabat-Zinn published a book called *Full Catastrophe Living*. The idea is that mindfulness meditation could help people to live with the full spectrum of pain – physical and mental – which human life entails. It would be hard to argue that having a child who is suffering is anything other than living the 'full catastrophe'.

There are many possible places to start practising mindfulness meditation, if it appeals – there's a dizzying array of different ways in. Many of these have now been monetised with apps, training courses and branded therapies. But ultimately, it's about paying attention. That takes a lot of practice and effort, but small positive changes can happen pretty quickly.

You are not alone: Stephanie's story

'Paying attention feels like letting yourself go right into what you're trying to escape from, instead of turning away. And that sort of helps you find your way through to another exit. You think it might get you stuck, but actually it does the opposite. I've found this in yoga, music, writing . . . Often you feel you should widen your gaze, when what you really need is to zoom in. When you stick with something, and examine it, you go deeper rather than cast about.'

Where to start

At the time of writing, streaming platforms freely offer tried and tested mindfulness meditation tracks. Jon Kabat-Zinn and Mark Williams both offer these, for example. If it's possible to set aside time in a day to sit, or lie, and follow the instructions in these tracks, that's a brilliant place to start. As Eckhart Tolle said, different ways people 'teach' mindfulness are just differences in the signposts, but should be leading in the same direction.

Often, it's helpful to set aside a specific time for regular formal practice. It can be as little as a few minutes if that's all you have, but longer periods – half an hour, perhaps – when you're starting out can be helpful. This can be to focus on a specific 'anchor' for attention, and using guided meditation tracks (like those Jon Kabat-Zinn makes available) can be a good start. The breath is a common 'anchor' – you might focus on simply feeling it entering and leaving your body. Different thoughts and feelings – often very difficult ones – will inevitably come up. And when they do, that's fine. *Anything* is fine. You just notice what's arisen, and gently bring your attention back to watching your breath without judging whatever's come up. You don't argue with the thoughts or feelings, or seek to label them as helpful or unhelpful. You just see them and let them pass.

Many people find regular practice changes their relationship with thoughts, and hones an ability to remain present and non-judgementally aware.

A few of the parents we spoke with talked about formal mindfulness (or a related type of) meditation practice as something which had helped them.

You are not alone: Petra's story

'When I was at my lowest about Alfie and it was all desperate, I was given a set of meditation CDs by a friend. At that point it felt like there was no way forward for Alfie or for me. That was a terrible time. Because I'd been given the CDs and I had heard they could help, I started with doing a 'body scan' meditation when I woke up during the night. For that one, you focus on sensations in different parts of your body. I also liked a shorter one where you focus on your breath. The instruction to let things arise and pass was incredibly difficult to follow, but I started to find moments when I could do that, briefly. Also, even though the instruction was to stay awake, it would sometimes get me to sleep. That was actually really useful. Practising every day definitely started to help. It's hard to put into words, but when you realise that all you ever have to deal with are specific moments – never more than that at one time – that's a major change.'

19: Accepting the contents of the present moment

Different metaphors have been suggested for mindful awareness and some people also find these helpful. Some advocate that you envisage passing thoughts as if they're leaves in a river. Some suggest that you see your field of awareness like the sky, and the experiences like changes in the weather which come and go.

Ultimately, the way of being which is fostered by formal meditation practice (or yoga, or similar) can affect attitudes and experiences throughout the rest of life.

Some see formal meditation practice as unnecessary, and are able to find their own anchor for awareness in the present moment through being absorbed in other experiences, and we give examples below. But many do find more formal guidance helps them to establish a way to practise.

Exercise 19.1: Mindfulness of breath

Mindfulness of breathing is often one of the first elements of mindfulness to practise. Your breath can be an 'anchor' to pay attention to – something that's always there with you, in the present moment.

Put aside a set period of time (10 minutes, 20 minutes . . . whatever you have available). Set a timer if you need to.

Lie down in a comfortable position or sit upright in a chair. Close your eyes.

Watch your breath.

Focus on a specific place where you can feel it most vividly. For some people, this might be in the nostrils; for others, it might be your abdomen.

Feel the breath going in and out. Notice the point where the in breath stops, and then the out breath begins.

Your mind will wander. You might start worrying, planning or judging yourself. When you notice this happen, gently bring your attention back to your breath. You'll do this again, and again and again. And this is OK.

Exercise 19.2: Body scan

Set aside 20 minutes, ideally when you won't be interrupted. Set a timer if you need to.

Lie down in the position which is most comfortable for you, with your head supported by a pillow or rolled up blanket, and close your eyes.

Start with the toes of your right foot – what can you feel? It might be coldness, tingling, possibly even pain. Or perhaps nothing at all. Whatever it is, just notice. Put all your attention into the toes of your right foot.

Then let your toes fade away from attention.

Move onto the bottom of your right foot . . .

Turn the spotlight of attention on each area of your body in turn, finishing with the top of your head.

Your attention will wander, and that's absolutely fine. But each time you notice this, gently bring your attention back to the part of the body you're currently focusing on.

Remember – the aim is just to notice and attend to what's going on. Whatever you experience – that's OK.

Exercise 19.3: Being the sky

Lie down in the position which is most comfortable for you, with your head supported by a pillow or rolled up blanket, and close your eyes.

Imagine that you are the sky.

Your thoughts are clouds. Don't try to hold onto them. Don't argue with them or question them. Just notice them.

Look at each one, and let it pass.

Sometimes there will be a storm – thoughts and emotions will be fierce, loud and drenching. There may be thunder and lightning.

You are not the clouds, the thunder or the lightning.

You are the sky, and all of this will pass.

Regular practice is the key

Learning to pay attention – to accept the moment – is a skill. It takes regular, consistent practice.

Research shows that doing regular practice can change people's relationship with their thoughts and emotions. There's evidence that it can help with a lot of different things, from mood difficulties (e.g., for people who've been diagnosed with depression or anxiety) to physical pain. It can also help with interactions with other people.

Reading about it can be useful (and there are lots of books out there). However, it's the practice which generally makes a real difference.

Some people find using specific apps on their phones useful. These can remind you to practise and provide audio tracks to guide you.

CHAPTER 19: SUMMARY AND KEY MESSAGES

- Regular practice with staying present/aware in the moment can lead to lasting change

- There are lots of apps and audio tracks available to help with this practice

- Coping with each individual moment is all we ever need to do

---

20: What does accepting my own experiences have to do with my child?

Learning to pay attention to and accept the present moment might not directly change the life situations we or our children find ourselves in. It can, though, strip away some of the layers of suffering associated with them.

Working on present-moment awareness can also have profound effects on people's interactions (and there's an increasing body of evidence for this).

One thing worth considering is how much and in what ways we share in all the – often distressing – things our child might be feeling. Our ability to empathise with other people's feelings – to feel them, to some extent, alongside them – is very important. It is crucial, in fact, to many normal interactions, including in parenting. When your child is happy, you share in that happiness. When your child is sad, you feel sadness, too. But sometimes when someone else is suffering a lot, empathy can tip into what some have called 'empathic distress'. This is when we're feeling others' pain to the degree that it can become draining and overwhelming. Many of the parents we spoke to for this book discussed experiences akin to this 'empathic distress'.

Matthieu Ricard, a Buddhist monk, and Tania Singer, a neuroscientist, demonstrated that under some circumstances, empathy (feeling *with* someone) can be very draining, and that this can be distinct from compassion (feeling *for* them).

Ricard, Singer and their colleagues ran experiments in which participants watched videos of other people who were suffering. Before watching these videos, they were first trained in 'empathy'. In 'empathy training', people practised really imagining intensely what the suffering of other people felt like, sometimes saying statements in their heads like 'I share your suffering' or 'I see your pain'. After this type of training people who watched the videos reported higher levels of negative emotions, and brain scans showed there was more activity in areas representing empathy for pain.

They then took part in something different, called 'compassion training'. Compassion training is based around 'loving-kindness' meditation, where warmth, friendliness and concern are fostered and directed towards oneself and others. Statements like 'may I be sheltered by compassion' or 'may I be safe' are used, and then people are instructed to extend this sentiment to people they are close to, as well as strangers. After this training, the effects of the previous 'empathy' training were reversed. People reported more positive emotions, and their brain activation was also different in ways consistent with this.

The 'empathy' (feeling *with*) training was experienced as extremely draining (by research participants and also by Ricard, when he tried it). One person reported that, after it, all she could see was human suffering. On the other hand, 'compassion' (feeling *for*) training, in the form of loving-kindness meditation, has often been experienced as revitalising and calming.

20: What does this have to do with my child?

It may be that compassion (which might well be cultivated by meditation) can help us to engage more fruitfully with our children's suffering, and not feel so overwhelmed by it. Some of the parents spoke about this, too.

This isn't to say that we should stop empathising. But with practice, it might be possible to cultivate awareness of how our feelings are affected by the feelings of our children, and to learn to direct compassion towards them as well as engaging empathically.

Another well-known Buddhist monk, Thich Nhat Hanh, has spoken about how listening to other people with compassion can ease *their* suffering.

There's also some evidence that practising being more aware of our own experiences can make us respond to intense emotion more calmly. The greater our awareness of how fear or anger (for example) feel, the more space we create to react in the way we want to, rather than automatically.

You are not alone: Petra's story

'I've got to know and recognise the feelings in my body, and how my thoughts speed up and whizz about when I'm getting really wound up. I sort of think, "Oh, it's this again". That can just give me a moment to take a breath and try to think what the best thing to do would be. It's less often now that I find myself shouting things I later regret at Alfie.'

So, in case you need more motivation even than the reduction in your own suffering, practising meditation (with all its implications for acceptance) is likely to help your child as well.

And anyway, it might help you to feel better. And that, on its own, is enough.

Exercise 20.1: Loving-kindness meditation

Loving-kindness meditation is a little different from meditation exercises which focus only on your direct experiences of breath or feelings in your body. The idea is that you concentrate a feeling of loving-kindness towards yourself and then towards other people. It can sometimes involve repeating phrases in your mind to foster loving kindness. There are different ways to do this (and, again, there are audio tracks online you can use).

Here's a start:

Lie down in the position which is most comfortable for you, with your head supported by a pillow or rolled up blanket, and close your eyes.

Bring to mind a person who really loves or loved you, and who accepts or accepted you just for who you are. Really feel – bask in – the love, wishes for wellbeing and happiness directed to you from that person. Remember – this love is for you, just as you are. You don't need to do anything to 'deserve' it. It just is. If you struggle with bringing to mind a real person here, you can envisage a person in your imagination.

Repeat, in your mind, 'May I be happy, may I be free from suffering, may I have ease of being'.

After remaining with this feeling of being embraced by loving kindness, you can then extend it to someone you love. Repeat, in your mind, 'May you be happy, may you be free from suffering, may you have ease of being'.

If you like, you can work towards extending the loving kindness further, towards people and creatures in the world more broadly. Again, repeat 'May you be happy, may you be free from suffering, may you have ease of being'.

Exercise 20.2: Mindful listening

This is Thich Nhat Hahn's definition of mindful listening:

'In mindful listening we listen with the sole purpose of helping the other person feel heard and accepted'

It can be surprising how little we actually *listen* to the people who talk to us. You might notice that often you're waiting for someone to finish speaking, so that you can offer an opinion, judgement or a defence of yourself. But true listening is something we can practise and learn. Learning to do this can help you feel more connected with other people, which can generally make you – and other people – feel better.

Sometimes, listening can be even harder when it's your child who's speaking. We're often so desperate to fix things for them, or to advise, or to remedy, remove or deny to ourselves any difficult feelings they might be experiencing. Don't expect to be able to always listen actively or to learn this all at once. It can be hard, and that's OK.

You might try this:

When speaking with a friend, practise really listening, without judgement, to them speaking to you. Make an active decision and effort to pay attention to what they're saying. Listen to their words, and what they're trying to communicate. Resist any temptation to interrupt, or to say what you think. Bring your active awareness to just hearing your friend speak.

You might also then try this with your child. Can you ask them a question (perhaps about how they are, or how their day has been), and then really pay attention to the answer?

Practising mindfulness (with the exercises above, for example) can help with this exercise, too. If you're able to accept your own emotional reactions to what your child says, you're likely to find it easier to let these pass without reacting in ways you don't want to.

You are not alone: Justine's story

'Ash was born female but is trans – he identifies as a boy. This was happening around the time Ash turned fourteen, just last year, though of course it's impossible to put a date on it. I'm still trying to learn to call him 'he' – it's so confusing. There are so many questions and I'm not sure even if it's OK to ask them. For instance, how long have I been loving Ash as my daughter when he's been thinking of himself as a son? And how does that matter? I feel that it shouldn't because he's obviously the same person I've always loved: my perfectly and beautifully unique child.

'But it's still really, really difficult, and I feel guilty about that, which doesn't help, but so often it's the small, even

petty things that trip you up when you're trying not to make a big deal of this. It feels wrong to be focused on these small details compared to the big issue of your child feeling accepted as how he wants to be recognised. So, I beat myself up for missing the jokes we had together as the two girls in the house, the stories we read and the secrets we shared and the common experiences I looked forward to talking about together because we shared particular characteristics. I feel selfish for feeling somehow rejected because Ash has not chosen, after all, the woman's life I live.

'So, I'm still struggling with this. I'm constantly trying to avoid putting too much emphasis on how other people will react, and bolstering his confidence and positivity about his body instead. But I don't know how realistic that is, or how fast people's perceptions can adapt in this changing environment. It's another thing that wrong-foots and confuses me – that I now feel even more protective of this son who I see as more vulnerable in certain ways than my daughter was. It's bewildering, trying to balance Ash's feelings, and mine, and society's of course.

'The only way I've found helps is to keep learning to look at Ash as just Ash – as he is right now. I look into his eyes and in that very moment I see and love the person Ash is, as I always have since the day he was born. And I've also learned to just listen more. Even if I have no idea what to say – I just listen. This is definitely a crash course in acceptance.'

CHAPTER 20: SUMMARY AND KEY MESSAGES

- Learning to stay present can help our interactions with other people, including our children

- Exercises in active listening, and 'loving-kindness meditation' can help us learn to stay present

- There can be a difference between 'feeling with' someone, which can be overwhelming, and 'feeling for' someone. This might include our children

21: What you might notice

Observing a feeling changes that feeling

Many people have found that really paying attention to their experiences (of anger, happiness, fear, grief or whatever arises) can change how these experiences feel. Although staying present with difficult emotions can be a big challenge, over time you might find you can watch them without feeling so caught up within them. You might even find that they aren't as constant or intolerable as they had sometimes seemed.

The problem with thinking

Practising meditation often allows us to notice certain things about thinking.

Thinking can be pretty useful. Our thinking minds are incredibly useful tools, in parenting and everything else. They've enabled us to invent the wheel, agriculture and modern medicine. They let us imagine and avoid the negative consequences of actions without experiencing them directly. They let us learn 'parenting tips' from each other through language as well as direct observation. When we're parents, we're particularly encouraged to look into the future on behalf of our children. So much of what we praise as 'good parenting' is about future consequences (eat right now to be healthy later; practise your piano now, so you can play in the future). And we're also often trying to find causes in the past, to learn from (are they behaving like that now because I got them up too early?).

Incompletely understood as they are (and there are *many* books, and reams of research on the topic), thinking minds are useful.

However, our everyday mental life doesn't always lead to a peaceful existence.

We probably all know what it's like to be unable to 'switch off' from thinking about our children's difficulties. Have you ever lain, sat or walked about unable to stop thinking about what's happened in your child's life, which you wish hadn't? Judging yourself as a parent? Comparing yourself to other people? Comparing your child with other people's children? Playing and replaying the things you 'shouldn't' have done; painfully imagining what you 'should' have done instead, but didn't? Wondering, on repeat, *why?* Imagining future worst-case scenarios? Trying to replace these worst-case scenarios with nicer images? Reasoning with yourself, yet again, to try to see the positives? Chastising yourself for seeing the problems more than the 'positive' qualities of your child? If you do experience this, you're far from alone. It's what thinking minds do.

You are not alone: Petra's story

'I couldn't begin to count the hours I've spent agonising about where things started to go wrong with Alfie. What did I do, when he was little, which might be a risk factor for diabetes and which might have made him not happy now? Could I have saved my marriage? I'd torture myself with this – thinking again and again about it. If Paul and I were still together, would Alfie still be at school now?

> *'It's hard not to imagine all the other bad stuff that might happen. What if he starts refusing his diabetes checks? What about when I can't force him to go to them? How will he cope if he gets complications?'*

It's also common to try very hard to actively break out of painful cycles of thinking, but not be able to.

As you'll have seen in previous chapters, many psychological techniques people find helpful are about challenging, testing and changing unhelpful thoughts and learning to develop and emphasise more helpful ones.

There's also evidence, though, that trying to grapple with/wrestle with our thoughts can sometimes (and perhaps particularly for some people) be counterproductive. In particular, we often get caught up in trying to control our thoughts in a way which sometimes just doesn't work.

You are not alone: Petra's story

'I'd get very low about all of this – what had gone wrong, what I'd done wrong, and how bad it might get. And then I'd get guilty about all the negative things I was thinking too – that I was seeing all these negatives about my son. Not being optimistic enough about him and how great he really is. I'd argue and argue with myself, but I couldn't seem to reason myself out of it. Learning to meditate was a turning point for me.'

Practising mindfulness is another possible way to deal with negative thinking. Rather than attempting to change our thought patterns, we might develop a different relationship with thinking. We can separate our perception of ourselves from the contents of our thoughts. We might see the limits of thought – and the narratives set up by it – in general.

Thinking as an addiction

Even thinking which isn't immediately painful (for example, patterns of thinking which lead to you feeling better about your actions and yourself, rather than worse) can arguably set up stories which restrict the world into the kind of structure which is intimately tied up with suffering. In fact, when thinking is pleasurable – when things are going well, and you can attach to thoughts like, 'He's getting better', or, 'Actually, I've done a pretty good job' – there's not much motivation to separate yourself from it. Because parenting is so much under the spotlight ('the world's most important job'), positive thoughts about it can feel bloody amazing. This all makes 'distancing from' thoughts more difficult to maintain, and many people find that it takes something very difficult (like a suffering child) to realise that the pleasurable elements of thinking are outweighed in the long run by the suffering associated with it.

Thoughts of blame, causation and yourself

We can get very caught up in assessing our specific impact in the world, and nowhere more so than in relation to our kids. It's not surprising. From before our kids' births, we're bombarded with messages about how important our actions are in 'getting it right'. Magazine articles and TV programmes with 'monster mums' feed on our desire to reassure ourselves, via flattering comparisons, that we're not doing too badly. Expensive products (from special baby foods to academic tutoring courses) are marketed to us on the basis that our buying them will lead to positive outcomes for our children.

You are not alone: Liz's story

'In the depths of night, I sometimes Google "worst parents in history", to bask in the relief that I (unlike the renowned Bulgarian countess Elizabeth Báthory) have never once abandoned my children in order to bathe in the blood of my murder victims. Nor do I anticipate tearing out chunks of my adult daughter's hair (like Catherine de Medici) if she has an affair.'

Academic research and the way it is reported is also interesting. Every year, hundreds of scientific articles are published linking specific behaviours of parents to some kind of desirable or undesirable 'outcome' in their children. 'Breast feeding associated with lower obesity rates.' 'Disruption to early attachment is associated with later mental illness.' We are encouraged to base actions around these pieces of information. It's hard not to fixate on the simplified models of the world this promotes.

This is a double-edged sword, as it can help us escape the unpredictability and uncontrollability of the world. But it can also lead to an overblown sense of blame by making us think we have more control than we really do. Neither the studies nor our minds are capable of dealing with the huge complexity of reality.

You are not alone: Petra's story

'Sometimes it's really useful to work out what you've done which is unhelpful, and how you can do it differently later. Alfie will sometimes tell me (not always politely, either) and I can think, "Yep, OK, that was a mistake". Like when I realised that he was so angry with me because I'd asked him about his insulin in front of a girl. I haven't done that again, and he told me the other day that he appreciates it. We've come up with some ways I can check in about it without him being embarrassed. Sitting down and deliberately thinking about how I can help Alfie control his diabetes can be really helpful. I've come up with recipes; I've thought of some brilliant ways for him to have a birthday party without me there, like he wants; I've negotiated how his dad can be involved without causing any aggro. But I almost never have the good ideas when I'm ruminating on all the guilt in the past or telling myself to buck up and deal with it. They often come in sideways when I'm out for a walk or something.'

You are not your child. This is both true, and – as we hope we've shown in Chapter 2 – important.

But arguably we tend to see ourselves as too separate from other people – and among other things, this encourages us to over-estimate our own lonely influence. We're very good at trying to work out all the many things which might be causing our children to struggle – things which they themselves can't be held accountable for. And we (along with the research literature) often consider ourselves or our actions as parents, as possible factors influencing our children's pain. But then we stop there, as if we ourselves are especially and uniquely to blame or in control; as if we're some kind of exception to the incredibly complicated way the world works. If we recognise that our children are affected by complex, uncontrollable, incomprehensible and invisible influences, why can't we admit we're no different? That this applies to us too? Sometimes, it's good to remember, in this world of individuality and specialness, that we're not so special. We're all just humans.

And here's the thing: we really can't know what our influence is going to be. Professor Yuko Munakata, a psychologist in America who specialises in child development, has likened the actions we take as parents to the butterfly that flaps its wings in one place and changes the weather on the other side of the world. We can have an effect, but it's far too complex for us to predict what that effect will be. The same action will have entirely different effects on different children, at different times, in different places. We just can't control it.

A change in perspective

Our minds like to keep us stuck at certain levels of thinking, often going round and round in loops about specific problems (like the ones about causes and blame above). And that's OK – it's just what minds do.

Sometimes, one of the things meditation can do is to help us 'shift levels', leaving the mind to just do its thing without getting caught in its sticky loops. Petra described this as 'zooming in or out' (see below).

For some people, religion helps, both with helping them feel connected with other people, and also with something beyond other people – a sense of placing things in the context of a broader universe, and of dimensions which we don't claim or attempt to understand.

You are not alone: Petra's story

'I'm getting much more practised at what I call "zooming out", now. It's the feeling you can get from looking up into the sky at night or staring out to sea. There's a sense of something bigger – the pain is real, but you can sort of feel it resonating as part of the rest of the world, and it doesn't feel like it's all about me anymore. There's also zooming in. When you just focus on something really detailed, like the feeling of breath coming in at your nose, something opens up.'

CHAPTER 21: SUMMARY AND KEY MESSAGES

- Paying attention to feelings changes those feelings

- Watching your patterns of thinking – including those about your children – can help to distance from them (they are 'just' thoughts!)

- We can practise learning to live with whatever comes our way, however difficult this is

22: Grief

When a child dies

Perhaps the most unacceptable thing of all is when a person's child dies. There are books aimed at this situation specifically, but it's worth touching on here.

The word 'acceptance' often comes up in the context of grief. Psychiatrist Elisabeth Kübler-Ross proposed a popular model of grief in the 1960s, which holds acceptance as the final of five 'stages' of grief: denial, anger, bargaining, depression and acceptance. Although it's been hugely influential, there's not a lot of research support for the model, and over the years it's been criticised repeatedly (including by Kübler-Ross herself). For a start, the 'five stages', if they occur, don't usually do so in sequence. But it's also increasingly obvious that this model of grieving is at odds in other ways with what many people experience. In particular, the way 'acceptance' is sometimes characterised implies that people might 'move on from', or (to some) 'get over' the loss.

Parents who have lost a child often point to their own or other people's expectations as complicating their experience of grief. And many parents whose children have died describe how the world around them isn't set up to acknowledge the fact that grief like this often never 'goes away', 'resolves', or settles into the type of 'acceptance' others might want it to. Dr Joanne Cacciatore, a researcher and also a bereaved mother says 'Others may tell us that it's time to "move on" or that this is a "part of some bigger plan" – because our shattering makes them feel uneasy, vulnerable, at risk'. She also writes that 'When others . . . push us toward healing before we are ready, they simply redouble our burden.'

Unfortunately, the medical and psychological professions sometimes talk in terms of illness. They use phrases like 'persistent complex related bereavement disorder', which sounds very scientific but, like many diagnostic categories, is backed by questionable evidence. This kind of label risks medicalising normal responses to deeply traumatic events and situations and can inflict unnecessary additional anxiety on top of natural, inescapable grief. Dr Cacciatore (drawing on her widely published research, personal experiences, experiences as a grief counsellor and engagement with Buddhist philosophy) emphasises the importance of allowing oneself to experience the storm of emotion traumatic bereavements entail.

You are not alone: Felicia's story

'My child died by suicide. In relation to grief, "accept-ance" has unfortunate connotations. An old friend of mine told me that her mother "never got over" the death of her eldest son. "She just could never accept it. She was never the same again.". I was terrified of this happening to me and my family. I read books about "complicated grief" and how to avoid it. But I soon started to realise that the very last thing I wanted was to "get over" my grief, even when it made me stop functioning. What I needed to do was to find where to keep it, because it was both part of

> *me and of my child, and it was a part of us which con-*
> *nected us, and which I would never want to let go. Grief is*
> *agonising and exhausting and ongoing, but I wouldn't be*
> *without it. It is my child and it is me. Acceptance for me*
> *means remaking myself bit by bit, because nothing will be*
> *the same again, and I wouldn't want it to be. Acceptance*
> *means I'll take my child and my grief safely with me*
> *always, living and loving, just as all my family have to. We*
> *all have to.'*

Grief for the living

Parents of children who are living but suffering also talk about different types of grief, albeit distinct from the grief of losing a child.

If your child is ill in a way which threatens their life, you may be experiencing grief in anticipation of possible death.

And if your child's experience of life is very difficult or traumatic to observe, this can involve what we might term grief as well. There's the loss of what you anticipated, hoped for and assumed for your child. This isn't a one-off event and can come to the fore repeatedly with changing life situations, birthdays, their friends' marriages . . . sometimes it can feel like there's a trigger for this in every social (and non-social) situation. Just as a child's death is unacceptable, and yet countless numbers of us must accept it every year, equally unacceptable is a child's suffering.

You are not alone: Benjamin's story

'When my daughter was at her lowest, I could see no way out for any of us. I thought she was going to end her life at some point, and I felt powerless to intervene. Her depression was too strong, and we were all sinking with it. I remember feeling that I was experiencing a living grief of sorts and it was torture for all of us. I could recognise nothing in her from the active and sunny child she had once been, I was grieving something that I felt had gone.'

Cacciatore points out that there's no way around grief – 'when we love deeply, we mourn deeply'. And the 'attending to grief' which she writes about may also apply (in different ways) to grief in the context of living children.

You are not alone: Diana's story

'I've definitely grieved for the Cassie we had before her accident. But I've learned how important it is for me to try not to always bring past expectations of Cassie to compare with how Cassie is now. Cassie is how she is now, and that will keep on changing, like everything else in life keeps on changing.'

CHAPTER 22: SUMMARY AND KEY MESSAGES

- Parents of a child who has died usually say the grief never goes away, but can change over time to something which can be lived with more easily

- Sometimes when a child is suffering or has changed a lot, there can be grief for living children as well. This is also likely to evolve over time and with changing circumstances. Even when situations don't fully resolve, the grief can become less acutely painful and easier to live with

23: Acceptance and action

We hope it's clear by now that acceptance isn't the same as resigna-tion. In fact, it's often when we experience moments of acceptance of 'what is' that we feel able to take the action we want to.

What's important to you?

There's a type of therapy called Acceptance and Commitment Therapy (ACT), which was initially developed by Steven Hayes and others. There's increasing evidence that this is a good approach for a lot of different issues, including when there's stuff in life which is difficult and not easily changed. So, there's lots which is relevant to being a parent when things are tough.

As the name suggests, ACT emphasises acceptance (of current experience).

But another thing it highlights is the importance of committing to acting in ways which are guided by your 'values'. Your values are the principles which you want to live by. Very simply, doing things – even small things – which are in line with our values can make us feel better.

Of course, there's a lot more to ACT than we can or would want to cover here (and working out values can sometimes not be straight-forward). But the idea of figuring out what's important to you and acting in ways which are led by this can be very useful.

So, what's really important to you? Values aren't goals or achievements. They're ideas or principles you'd like to guide how you
live your life on an ongoing basis. Some people might find their
strongest values relate to being kind, or honest, or hard working or
disciplined. For others, being creative, forgiving or fun might be
at the forefront. Spirituality may be an important value for some.
And of course, many of your values are probably very relevant to
how you want to act as a parent. If being respectful is important to
you, for example, how might this manifest in your parenting? And
what can you do to help this respectfulness affect how you are with
your child? But there are probably also many other ways you can
act in line with your values which might not involve your children
at all. If you value being caring, might that also lead to giving to an
animal charity? Maybe valuing your romantic side would mean you
remember and mark your wedding anniversary?

When you're feeling overwhelmed by the task of caring for a child
who's unhappy, it can be easy to feel your world is shrinking.
Identifying what your values are and thinking how to express them
by bringing them, just in small ways, into the different corners of
your life, can be helpful.

Exercise 23.1: Reflecting on your values

You might find it useful to spend a few minutes thinking about
what values matter to you. They may be things you feel have
evolved over time, or perhaps there are some which you feel have
been part of who you are from childhood onwards, long before
you were a parent.

Write some down here:

....

....

....

....

....

....

If you have a value related to being thoughtful, and you have five minutes and the energy, perhaps you can send a text message to the friend who's going to the job centre today. If you have a value about nurturing life, and you're able to, you might water the spider plant or put out some bird seed.

You don't have to do anything massive. You don't have to 'achieve' anything. And sometimes, it'll be impossible to do anything at all – that's fine, too. But being aware of your values can help you do small things which are in line with them, and that can remind you to feel like you, even while the storms rage.

Connectedness

Often, people find that acting in line with their values can involve connecting with other people. But this can also be really hard.

Most people we spoke with for this book had felt very alone. Some talked about how worries about judgement or blame (which we mentioned earlier), and a sense that other people aren't going through the same or don't understand, have sometimes prevented them from wanting to be around other people. We've all experienced this in some form.

A sense of aloneness, and of feeling disconnected from other people, may be growing (certainly in 'Western' society) by the generation. And feeling separated from other people can wallop our mental wellbeing.

That's one of the things we've learned when talking to other people about this book. So many people are going through something like this, and so many people don't know how, where or whether to talk about it.

One thing about practising accepting whatever you're going through is that it can make it easier to connect with other people about it, too.

Who can you be sad with? As we've seen above, we're often not kind to our own negative emotions. And society's not kind to negative emotion, rewarding the kind of positivity which is sometimes just not possible (and may not be desirable). It can be helpful to keep an eye out for and notice people you don't have to pretend with.

For some people, animals can be the best at this. Joanne Cacciatore, who we talked about earlier, has said that one of the best therapists she's encountered is a horse who'd been through a lot of trauma with a previous owner. Parents would find that they could remain present with this horse, that they could feel whatever they felt in his accepting presence, and that they were soothed.

You are not alone: Elena's story

'When my daughter was at her worst, I mostly avoided people. I just felt like no one could understand. But there were some exceptions. A woman at work – one of the secretaries – just seemed to get it. I never felt like I had to pretend, and she always just quietly made me a cup of tea. I discovered quite recently that she'd had a child who was stillborn about thirty years earlier. I wonder whether that's why she understood something about pain.'

CHAPTER 23: SUMMARY AND KEY MESSAGES

- Working out and committing to your values, and doing what's important to you, can be very helpful. What's important to you might include your child(ren), but often there's a lot else, too

- For many people, this involves connecting with other people. Keep an eye out for the positive connections in your life

24: Growing

No one would choose to go through their child struggling. We really don't want to say anything glib about suffering making you stronger.

But sometimes people say that going through difficulties like these can teach us important lessons. Some people have spoken about learning from such intensely hard times about what truly matters in our lives, about our imperfections, or about how there are never any guarantees. Importantly, people have told us about how they were able to tolerate far more than they thought they could. Many people we spoke to felt that they had learned from their difficulties in some way.

You are not alone: Petra's story

'I really hate that phrase, "What doesn't kill you makes you stronger". There have been times when I've felt the absolute opposite – that some of the problems I've faced with Alfie have really broken me down – made me weak.

'But I have to admit that there have also been some times recently when I've felt a bit in awe of how I've been able to manage. I'm still here, still breathing. And if I let myself realise it, I have learned a huge amount. I really don't spend my life worrying about the future or obsessing about the past in the same way anymore. I can see that "now" is all any of us ever has.'

You are not alone: Elena's story

'I'm not the same person as I was a few years ago, and actually a lot of that change is positive. I've learned never to judge other people's situations. I'm a much better listener. I wouldn't have chosen what we've had to go through, but it's made us all who we are.'

The research supports the idea that our struggles and challenges can bring some positives alongside them. There is even a name for it – 'post-traumatic growth', which is the positive psychological change that some individuals experience after a life crisis or traumatic event. Connecting with other people, discovering what is really important in life and, sometimes, discovering forms of spirituality can be part of this.

The concept doesn't deny deep distress, but rather describes how adversity can unintentionally yield changes in understanding oneself, others and the world.

Guesthouse poem (Rumi)

This being human is a guest house.
Every morning a new arrival.
A joy, a depression, a meanness,
some momentary awareness comes
as an unexpected visitor.
Welcome and entertain them all!
Even if they're a crowd of sorrows,
who violently sweep your house

empty of its furniture,
still, treat each guest honourably.
He may be clearing you out
for some new delight.
The dark thought, the shame, the malice,
meet them at the door laughing,
and invite them in.
Be grateful for whoever comes,
because each has been sent
as a guide from beyond.

Exercise 24: What you have learned

Think about whether there have been any small 'silver linings' to the challenges you have found yourself facing. It may be that you have learned parenting techniques that benefit your other children, it may be that you have learned how to listen. List as many as you can, in as much detail as you can. If you are struggling to think of anything, then write down what advice you would give to another parent in the same situation as you – this will show you all the learning that you have managed to achieve along your journey.

....

....

....

CHAPTER 24: SUMMARY AND KEY MESSAGES

- No one would choose to go through their child suffering. However, many people say they have 'grown' from the experience

- Sometimes, it can be helpful to reflect on what you've learned or how you've grown from the difficulties you've faced

SECTION 5:
OVERVIEW SUMMARY AND KEY MESSAGES

- Acceptance of one's own experiences and reactions – whatever they are – can have far-reaching positive effects

- Regular practice of mindfulness, using whatever approaches work best for you, can be central to this

- Working out what's important to you and acting in line with these values when you can, can help

- Although no one would choose it, we can learn a lot when things are tough

25: Final thoughts

Thank you for reading this book. And thank you to everyone who so generously shared their experiences. Although we don't know the details of what you and your child are going through right now, we are sure that the reason that you are struggling is because you love your child. If you didn't, it wouldn't be so painful, and you wouldn't have read a book about how to cope with the impact it has on you. Parenting can be extremely hard, and caring can be exhausting and difficult. It should definitely come with a health warning.

We met and spoke with a huge range of parents while writing this book, and the conversations were extremely honest, often very painful, and had moments of shared humour too. We were struck by the wide range of challenges that people face, and the many ways people manage to survive. Sometimes, two people's coping methods were completely opposite to each other. This brought home to us that there are no 'right' answers – because different things work for different people – and that everyone's circumstances are unique and constantly changing. We know that the chapters are different in subject matter and that the stories have a lot of different messages, but we think they complement each other. Common themes emerged, like building on your strengths, exploring ways to protect your own psychological well-being, using techniques to change your way of thinking, feeling and behaving, keeping other aspects of your life going and getting involved in the outside world, using what you've learnt to help other people, nurturing other family and social relationships, giving things time, and being kind to yourself.

By combining real stories with strategies from psychological research, we hope we have given you some ideas, tools and techniques to use and adapt to your own needs. We hope that the book brings comfort in the knowledge you are not alone, provides strategies that help you cope, and gives a sense of hope for the future.

Further resources

Below are some example resources that might be useful. They are focused on the UK as the authors are from the UK, but there are likely to be equivalent resources in your country or even more locally. When finding resources, it is really important to make sure that they are reliable, and are backed up by research evidence. Only use reputable resources such as those from the World Health Organization, your Centre for Disease Control, or national organisations with Government funding.

Parenting a child with school refusal

Not Fine in School (https://notfineinschool.co.uk/) A parenting website that many parents have mentioned, that is a fairly recent addition to the support landscape.

Parenting a child with autism

National Autistic Society (https://www.autism.org.uk) The **National Autistic Society** is the leading UK charity for **autistic** people (including those with Asperger syndrome) and their families. They provide information, support and pioneering services, and campaign for a world that works for **autistic** people.

Parenting a child with a mental health problem

The **Rollercoaster Parent Support** (https://search3.openobjects. com/mediamanager/durham/fsd/files/rollercoaster_support_flyer. pdf) project provides a programme of support to parents and carers of children and young people aged nought to twenty-five with emotional or mental health issues. It has an active Facebook support group that is linked to professional services as well as in-person meetings.

Alderson, S. (2020). *Never Let Go: How to Parent Your Child Through Mental Illness*, Vermillion.

Addressing mental health problems in yourself or your child

The **Overcoming** book series (https://overcoming.co.uk) from Robinson is an excellent place to find materials on addressing common mental health problems. Books include further information on coping as well as books on anxiety, depression, low self-esteem and body image. The series also includes books on helping your child overcome difficulties such as worrying.

Reading Well (https://reading-well.org.uk/books/books-on-pre scription) helps you to understand and manage your health and well-being using helpful reading. The books are chosen by health experts and people living with the conditions covered. People can be recommended a title by a health professional, or they can visit their local library and take a book out for free.

Charities are a good place to start, e.g., **YoungMinds** (https:// youngminds.org.uk/) and **Contact** (a charity for families with disabled children https://contact.org.uk/). Please do be aware of emergency helplines such as the 999 or 911 for emergency services in a life-threatening situation.

Books on grief

Cacciatore, J. (2017). *Bearing the Unbearable: Love, Loss, and the Heartbreaking Path of Grief*, Simon & Schuster.

Books and resources on Acceptance and Commitment Therapy

Hayes, S. C. (2005). *Get Out of Your Mind and Into Your Life: The New Acceptance and Commitment Therapy*, New Harbinger Publications.

Harris, R. (2008). *The Happiness Trap: Stop Struggling, Start Living*, Robinson.

Introductory website: https://stevenchayes.com/category/acceptance-and-commitment-therapy/

Worksheets from Russ Harris (including on working out your values): https://thehappinesstrap.com/upimages/Complete_Worksheets_2014.pdf

Books and resources on compassion-focused therapy

Gilbert, P. (2010). *The Compassionate Mind*, Robinson.

Resources for mindfulness practice

Streaming platforms offer many different types of audio tracks to help with practice. It can be helpful to look up introductory resources and courses from established practitioners.

Jon Kabat-Zinn's resources: https://www.mindfulnesscds.com/

Sam Harris's Waking Up website: https://wakingup.com/

Mark Williams's website: https://www.oxfordmindfulness.org/people/mark-williams/

Thich Nhat Hanh talks: https://thichnhathanhfoundation.org/covid-resources-dharmatalks

General

Wincer, P. (2020). *Tender: The Imperfect Art of Caring*, Coronet.
Thoughtful, subtle book exploring the range of emotions surrounding caring in all its guises. Supports much of what we are looking at.

Solomon, A. (2012). *Far from the Tree – Parents, Children and the Search for Identity*, Simon & Schuster.
Looks at the fairly taboo subject of struggling to find connection with your child with a very well researched and case study illustrated approach.

Acknowledgements

We would like to acknowledge the support of friends, colleagues, patients, parents and relatives who so generously shared their stories and inspired us to write the book.

Index

Note: page numbers in *italics* refer to diagrams.

Index

Index